G000060709

Published by
LINEA RECTA LIMITED

CONTENTS

INTRODUCTION

An account of God is a theory about what God is and what it means for God to be that. This particular account of God argues that God is supernatural and explains what it means for God to be supernatural. The account of God is natural in that it proceeds by natural means, i.e., means that are in accordance with contemporary methods and standards of rationality, as they are used in the natural sciences, as opposed to supernatural means, e.g., divine revelation.

Part I of the account is purely philosophical, non-sectarian. It argues that God is supernatural (or, to put it more precisely, that what is not supernatural, is not what is God) and discusses the direct implications of God being supernatural. It may seem rather 'dry' but is also quite revealing. For example: Given that God is supernatural, it shows that there cannot be more than one God, that God is referentially equivalent with some very familiar notions, and that God exists. It also explains the fundamental difference between God and all else (in metaphysical-ontological, logical-categorical, conceptual-epistemological, and ethical terms). In the Part I, each chapter builds on the previous, so it is important to start at the beginning.

Part II checks if the purely philosophical, non-sectarian account of God as supernatural, as developed in Part I, is still an account of God. In other words, it checks if I did not get lost in mere abstractions. It does so by checking if the typical attributes of the God of Abraham (of Judaism, Christianity, and Islam) and of the Godhead of the Vedas (of Hinduism), and even of the Tao (of Taoism) and of the Unborn, Deathless, Unconditioned (of Buddhism), cohere with the purely philosophical, non-sectarian account of God of Part I. In the process, Part II links the purely philosophical, non-sectarian account of God as supernatural to the theological, sectarian accounts of God as found in holy scriptures and elsewhere.

The next chapter checks if the account is successful. That is, if the basic idea that underlies the account (i.e., that God is supernatural) is readily and widely acceptable (i.e., intuitive and not *prima facie* contradictory), if the account is coherent (i.e., a unified whole, internally and externally consistent), and if the account is complete (i.e., covers all angles). I believe the account of God as supernatural meets these criteria. In addition, it has certain other important advantages over the doctrine of divine simplicity, perfect being theology, and other accounts of God.

The appendices provide some (sometimes more technical) notes. One appendix explains how the account bridges the apparent gap between natural and supernatural theology and philosophy. The last, extended appendix argues that the account of God as supernatural is fully compatible with the idea that God is simple (provided it means absolutely simple) and that God is perfect (provided it means absolutely perfect) yet has important advantages over the doctrine of divine simplicity and over perfect being theology. Another appendix explains the beauty of a supernatural God: That only a supernatural God truly qualifies as God. That only a supernatural God is truly infinite, supreme, greater-than-the-greatest. That only a supernatural God is truly perfect (i.e., complete and flawless). And that if we try to turn God into something more than just supernatural, we actually turn God into something less, something natural, the worship of which is idolatry.

I cannot but hope that this may help you to attain salvation, divine union, enlightenment, liberation, wisdom, or whatever you call *that* which sets you free. Free from sin and the consequences of sin, free from separation, free from craving and ignorance and the pain it causes, free from the cycle of birth and death and its suffering, or, to put it in somewhat plainer terms, free from the stress that comes from being deceived by appearances.

PART I

THAT GOD IS SUPERNATURAL AND WHAT IT MEANS FOR GOD TO BE SUPERNATURAL

Part I of the account of God as supernatural is purely philosophical, non-sectarian.

In chapter 1, I argue that God is supernatural. In chapter 2 to 5, I discuss some immediate implications of God being supernatural. In chapter 6 to 8, I present three familiar notions that are referentially equivalent with God as supernatural. These help to make the apparently abstract notion of God as supernatural concrete. In chapter 9 to 11, I explain that God *is* (i.e., exists, is real) and that God is essential, and good.

1. GOD IS SUPERNATURAL

In this chapter, I will argue that God is supernatural, explain what 'supernatural' means, and discuss some immediate implications of God being supernatural. If these implications seem trivial, please note that there are many people who believe that God is supernatural yet reject some of these implications. By stating these apparently trivial implications, I hope to cover the matter from all angles and avoid misunderstandings.

The basic proposition

The basic proposition (i.e., idea) underlying this account of God is that:

[1]   What is not supernatural, is not what is God.

Statement [1] is just one way of expressing the proposition. There are many other statements that can be used to express the same proposition. For example, 'Being supernatural is a necessary condition for being God', 'If X is God, X is supernatural', '(X is God) → (X is supernatural)', and so on.

In practice, I will often use simplified (contrapositive) versions of statements like statement [1]. In this case:

[1']   God is supernatural.

Whenever I use such simplified versions, they should be taken to stand for the original statement and express the same proposition. The simplified version is used for the sake of brevity and readability. The original versions are used to prevent confusion about existential import and circularity. For more on this, please see Appendix 5.

The basic idea is widely and readily acceptable

That God is supernatural may well be the only notion of God that is shared universally, applies to all Gods, and even appears to be necessarily true.

Practically everybody considers God to be supernatural, regardless of whether they believe that God exists, and regardless of whatever else they may also take God to be. With everybody, I mean everybody who has any familiarity at all with the term 'God'. Not just theists (who believe that God exists), but also atheists (who believe that God does not exist), agnostics (who believe that we cannot know if God exists), ignostics (who believe that the term 'God' is not sufficiently clear to discuss its existence), and even people who have not given the matter any serious thought at all.

The principal disagreement between theists, atheists, and agnostics is not about whether God is supernatural –although they may disagree about the ways in which God is supernatural and to what extent– but about whether (it can be known if) the notion of God is instantiated, i.e., whether God also exists in some other way than as a mere notion. Even ignostics do not deny that God is supernatural. They merely point out that there is no consensus on whatever else God is also taken to be.

All Gods are supernatural, at least in some ways. Not just the Abrahamic God(s), e.g., Yahweh / Jehovah, Allah, Elohim / Adonai; but also the Hindu God(s), e.g., Brahman, Brahma, Vishnu, Shiva; the Greek and Roman Gods, e.g., Zeus, Jupiter; and others, like Aten, Baha, Waheguru, Ahura Mazda, and so on. Even the ultimates of non-theistic religions are supernatural, e.g., the Tao of Lao Tzu and the deathless-unborn-unconditioned of the Buddha.

In fact, that God is supernatural seems to be true by definition, necessarily, by virtue of the meaning of the words, so it can be known with certainty. (In more technical, philosophical terms, we could argue that the proposition is analytic and that it can be known *a priori*.)

So, the idea that God is supernatural is shared universally, applies to all Gods, and even seems to be necessarily true. But do we really know what it means? Let us have a look at what 'supernatural' means.

9

What does ‘supernatural’ mean?

‘Supernatural’ literally means ‘outside and above the natural’. ‘Super-’ comes from Latin *super*, probably from Pre-Italic or Proto-Indo-European *eks-uper*, *eks*, meaning ‘out of’, and *uper*, meaning ‘over’, so I take super to mean ‘outside and above’. ‘Natural’ comes from Latin *natus*, meaning ‘born’, which I take in the usual wider sense of ‘born, created, caused, or otherwise conditioned’. Subsequently, ‘super-natural’ means outside and above the natural, outside and above all that is born, created, caused, or otherwise conditioned.

Here are some notes, just to avoid misunderstandings:

(a) ‘Natural’ does not just refer to ‘wild nature’, as opposed to humans and/or human creations, but includes both.

(b) So-called paranormal or preternatural phenomena, like extrasensory perception, precognition, telepathy, reincarnation, clairvoyance, psychokinesis, telekinesis, and so on, are not supernatural, but natural (i.e., conditioned, e.g., in time, space, causality), if perhaps strange and unexplained.

I don't agree

(c) ‘Supernatural’ does not mean ‘celestial’. So-called celestial phenomena, like angels, ghosts, spirits, demons, are not supernatural, but natural (i.e., conditioned, e.g., temporal, spatial, causal), if perhaps strange and unexplained.

I don't agree

(d) Ad (b) and (c): ‘Supernatural’ does not refer to any phenomena at all because all phenomena are conditioned and thus natural, and not supernatural, at least not under my definition of the terms.

? what does phenomena mean then?

(e) With ‘conditioned’, I mean ‘depending on conditions, circumstances, or anything else’. ‘Unconditioned’ means the opposite, that is, ‘not depending on conditions, circumstances, or anything else’. Subsequently, what is unconditioned, is also unconditional.

(f) The primary sense seems to have shifted over time from usually meaning "beyond" to usually meaning "very much," which can be contradictory. E.g. supersexual, which is attested from 1895 as "transcending sexuality," from 1968 as "very sexual."

It seems to me that you have decided that God is supernatural but nothing else is.

Are Miracles Supernatural?

What does it mean for God to be supernatural?

In this section, I will discuss some implications of God being supernatural.

1.1. God is outside and above the natural

That God is supernatural, means that God is outside and above the natural because 'super-natural' means 'outside and above the natural'.

1.1.1. God is outside and above all that is born, created, caused, conditioned

That God is supernatural, outside and above the natural, means that God is outside and above all that is born, created, caused, or otherwise conditioned because 'natural' means 'born, created, caused, or otherwise conditioned'.

does natural mean this?

1.1.1.1. God is outside and above all else

That God is supernatural, outside and above the natural, outside and above all that is born, created, caused, or otherwise conditioned, means that God is outside and above all else because all else is born, created, caused, or otherwise conditioned. For example:

God is outside and above all that is physical and/or mental

That God is supernatural, outside and above the natural, outside and above all that is born, created, caused, or otherwise conditioned, means that God is outside and above all that is physical and/or mental because all that is physical and/or mental is born, created, caused, or otherwise conditioned. In other words, that God is supernatural, means that God is not just super-physical, but also super-mental.

What does mental mean?

God is outside and above all that is subject to space, time, causality

That God is supernatural, outside and above the natural, outside and above all that is born, created, caused, or otherwise conditioned, means that God is outside and above space, time, and causality because space, time, and causality are born, created, caused, or otherwise conditioned. God is not spatial, has no dimensions, location, size, shape, form, etc. God is not temporal, has no duration, no beginning or end. God is not causal, neither cause nor effect, not a causal factor, not a link in the causal chain of events. Space, time, and causality themselves are conditioned, if only because they can be distinguished from each other.

Space, time is one thing. Causality is something else

1.1.1.2. God is outside and above all things

That God is supernatural, outside and above the natural, outside and above all that is born, created, caused, or otherwise conditioned, means that God is outside and above all things because all things are born, created, caused, or otherwise conditioned.

Notes:
(a) With 'all things', I mean all phenomena, all that appears (regardless of whether it also exists in some other way than as an appearance), e.g., physical (e.g., the world, the body), mental (e.g. thoughts, feelings, perceptions), and any supposed function(ing) thereof (e.g., the sense faculties); static (i.e., entities) and dynamic (i.e., events, processes); real and illusory (e.g., in waking life as well as in dreams); all that is conditioned (e.g., in time, space, and/or causality); all that can be determined, all (that has) distinguishing features, all (that has) properties, all (that belongs in the) categories, all genera and all of which genera can be predicated, all that can be defined categorically, all conceptual attributes and all concepts they belong to, all that can be conceptualized (i.e., conceived), all that is conceivable. Even if you believe in abstract things like numbers that exist outside of space and time, these numbers are conditioned phenomena – or else they could not be distinguished from each other. *I don't understand that.*

We could sum up section 1.1.1 by saying that it argues that 'God' and 'all else/all things' are mutually exclusive and jointly exhaustive complements in 'all'.

what does this mean?

1.2. God is not natural

That God is supernatural, outside and above the natural, means that God is not natural.

1.2.1. God is not born, created, caused, or otherwise conditioned

That God is supernatural, outside and above the natural, not natural, means that God is not born, not created, not caused, not otherwise conditioned.

1.2.1.1. God is not like anything else

That God is supernatural, outside and above the natural, not natural, not born, not created, not caused, not otherwise conditioned, means that God is not like anything else because all else is born, created, caused, or otherwise conditioned. For example:

God is neither physical nor mental

That God is supernatural, outside and above the natural, not natural, not born, not created, not caused, not otherwise conditioned, means that God is neither physical nor mental because all that is physical and/or mental is born, created, caused, or otherwise conditioned.

God is neither temporal, nor spatial, nor causal

That God is supernatural, outside and above the natural, not natural, not born, not created, not caused, not otherwise conditioned, means that God is neither temporal, nor spatial, nor causal because all that is spatial, temporal, and/or causal is born, created, caused, or otherwise conditioned. God is non-spatial, non-temporal, and non-causal.

1.2.1.2. God is not like a thing

That God is supernatural, outside and above the natural, not natural, not born, not created, not caused, and not otherwise conditioned, means that God is not like a thing because all things are born, created, caused, or otherwise conditioned.

1.3. Anything that is natural, is not God

That God is supernatural, outside and above the natural, not natural, means (by the kind of inference called contraposition) that anything that is natural, is not God.

This claim has the same meaning as (i.e., is logically equivalent with) the claims of the previous sections, but the emphasis is different. For example, where the last section stressed the fact that God is not natural, this section stresses the fact that anything that is natural is not God. In other words, in this section, we start by looking at natural things, and then deny that any of those things is God.

1.3.1. Anything that is born, created, caused, or otherwise conditioned, is not God

That God is supernatural, outside and above the natural, not natural, not born, created, caused, or otherwise conditioned, means that anything that is born, created, caused, or otherwise conditioned is not God.

1.3.1.1. Anything else is not God

That God is supernatural, outside and above the natural, not natural, not born, created, caused, or otherwise conditioned, means that anything else is not God because all else is born, created, caused, or otherwise conditioned. For example:

Anything that is physical and/or mental, is not God

That God is supernatural, outside and above the natural, not natural, not born, created, caused, or otherwise conditioned, means that anything that is physical and/or mental, is not God because all that is physical (e.g., bodies) and/or mental (e.g., thoughts, feelings, perceptions) is born, created, caused, or otherwise conditioned.

Anything that is subject to space, time, or causality, is not God

That God is supernatural, outside and above the natural, not natural, not born, created, caused, or otherwise conditioned, means that anything that is subject to space, time, and/or causality, is not God because all that is subject to space, time, and/or causality is born, created, caused, or otherwise conditioned.

1.3.1.2. No thing is God

That God is supernatural, outside and above the natural, not natural, not born, created, caused, or otherwise conditioned, means that no thing is God because all things are born, created, caused, or otherwise conditioned.

Notes:
(a) That God is not a thing, is sometimes expressed as 'God is nothing'. But this can easily cause confusion, depending on how 'nothing' is understood. If 'nothing' is understood as 'something that does not exist', then the claim that 'God is nothing' is not correct. (In fact, it seems self-contradictory because it suggests that there exists something that does not exist.)
(b) That God is not a thing (i.e., neither any thing in particular nor merely all things) and does not exist in the way that things exist, does not mean that God does not exist. For example, that God is not an object and does not exist in the way objects appear to exist, does not mean that God does not exist as the subject (in the 'thinnest' sense of the word).

[handwritten: 1st mention this possibly]

[handwritten: what does this mean?]

1.4. Other implications of God being supernatural

1.4.1. God is not born, so God cannot die

That God is supernatural, means that God is not born and thus cannot die, not created and thus cannot be destroyed, not caused and thus cannot disappear into its effect, and not otherwise conditioned and thus cannot change

1.4.2. God is not subject to the laws of nature

That God is supernatural, outside and above the natural, not natural, means that God is not subject to the "laws of nature" because the "laws" of nature only "govern" the natural. Thus, God seems to defy the laws of nature.

1.4.3. God is unconditioned, unconditional, absolute

That God is supernatural, outside and above the natural, not natural, not conditioned, means that God is unconditioned, and thus unconditional, or in one word absolute. ⟵ *This is a step too far,*

Notes:
    (a) 'Absolute' comes from the Latin *absolutus*, from *absolvere*, from *ab-*, meaning 'from, off' and *solvere*, meaning 'to loosen, untie, release, detach, set free from', and means 'unconditioned' and (thus) 'unconditional'. (So, yes, the absolute absolves!)

I do not see how GOD is absolute from what has been said so far.

1.4.4. God does not have (real, natural) properties

That God is supernatural, outside and above the natural, not natural, means that God does not have (real, natural) properties because only natural things have (real, natural) properties and because all (real, natural) properties are natural things.

Notes:
   (a) With 'properties', I mean distinguishing features, things that
       distinguish some things from other things, things that can truly be
       predicated of (the things denoted by) a subject-term, things that give
       the subject-term intensional meaning, *Sinn*, 'sense', qualitative identity.
   (b) It may well be that things are nothing but their properties. After all, if a
       thing is stripped of all of its properties, what is left of the thing?

1.4.5. God does not have a nature (i.e., essential properties)

That God is supernatural, outside and above the natural, not natural, and has no
properties, means that God does not have a nature, i.e., a (set of) essential
properties. Thus, the popular question 'What is the nature of God?' is invalid: it
presupposes that God has a nature, but God does not have a nature.

to speak about nature in this way is different to the use of natural ~ supernatural.

Summary of the chapter

1. God is supernatural
   - 1.1. God is outside and above the natural
     - 1.1.1. God is outside and above all that is born, created, caused, conditioned
       - 1.1.1.1. God is outside and above all else
         - God is outside and above the physical and mental
         - God is outside and above space, time, and causality
       - 1.1.1.2. God is outside and above all things
   - 1.2. God is not natural
     - 1.2.1. God is not born, created, caused, conditioned
       - 1.2.1.1. God is not like anything else
         - God is neither physical nor mental
         - God is neither in time, nor in space, nor in causality
       - 1.2.1.2. God is not like a thing
   - 1.3. Anything that is natural, is not God
     - 1.3.1. Anything that is born, created, caused, conditioned, is not God
       - 1.3.1.1. Anything else is not God
         - Anything that is physical and/or mental, is not God
         - Anything that is subject to space, time, or causality, is not God
       - 1.3.1.2. No thing is God
   - 1.4. Other implications of God being supernatural
     - 1.4.1. God is not born, so God cannot die
     - 1.4.2. God is not subject to the laws of nature
     - 1.4.3. God is unconditioned, unconditional, absolute
     - 1.4.4. God does not have (real, natural) properties
     - 1.4.5. God does not have a nature (i.e., essential properties)

2. GOD IS TRANSCATEGORICAL

In this chapter, I will explain what I mean with 'transcategorical', and then show that, given that God is (ontologically speaking) supernatural, God is (logically speaking) transcategorical, and then discuss some implications of God being transcategorical.

This is step 2 of the philosophical, non-sectarian, 'dry' account of God as supernatural.

The claim that 'God is transcategorical' is the simplified (contrapositive) version of the statement that 'what is not transcategorical, is not what is God'. Thus, it should not be taken to imply that God exists. (In logical terms, it lacks existential import.)

What does 'transcategorical' mean?

'Transcategorical' literally means 'beyond the categorical'. 'Trans-' comes from Latin *trans*, meaning 'across, beyond, on the other side of', which I consider to be synonymous with 'super-'. 'Categorical' comes from Latin *categoricus*, from the Greek verb *kategorein*, meaning 'to speak against, to accuse, to predicate, to sentence, to attribute, to ascribe'. The ancient Greek philosopher, Aristotle, borrowed the term from legal practice to build his (categorical) logic, based on predicating certain categories of other categories. Even today, a 'predicate expression' accuses the subject-term of belonging in a certain category (aka 'genus'). For example, the sentence, 'Socrates is a man', accuses Socrates of belonging in the category of men. Also, the default ('proper') way to define a term is still by predicating *genera* (accusing the term of belonging in particular categories) and *differentiae* (accusing the term of differing from other terms belonging in the same category). For example, the definition of bird could be, 'animal with wings', accusing a bird of belonging in the category of animals, and accusing a bird of differing from other animals in that it has wings. Aristotle intended the categories to categorize all things (i.e., all except being qua being), and, for the purposes of this paper, I will assume that the categories are indeed successful in categorizing all things. Thus, with 'transcategorical' I mean outside and above the categories, outside and above all genera (and thus also outside and above all differentiae), outside and above all predicates.

Notes:
(a) I use the terms 'genus' and 'category', and their plurals, 'genera' and 'categories', interchangeably.
(b) 'Differentiae' is the plural of 'differentia'.
(c) A (real, categorical) predicate consists of a genus, and possibly a differentia.
(d) A genus by itself, without differentia, is a (real, categorical) predicate, but a differentia by itself, without a genus, is not a (real, categorical) predicate.
(e) Although it is more accurate to say that 'predicates are predicated of subject-terms', for the sake of brevity and readability, I will often simply say that 'things have predicates'.

God is transcategorical

That God is supernatural, means that God is transcategorical. There are different ways to argue for this point. Here are two.

Rationale 1: Exactly and unconditionally the same.

Although the terms, 'supernatural' and 'transcategorical', may seem to have a different intensional meaning (i.e., *Sinn*, 'sense', qualitative identity), they have the exact same extensional meaning (i.e., *Bedeutung*, 'reference', numerical identity). To explain this, let us momentarily drop the prefixes, 'super-' and 'trans-', and start with the stems, 'natural' and 'categorical':
1. The intensional meaning of 'natural' is 'born, created, caused, or otherwise conditioned', and since all things are born, created, caused, or otherwise conditioned, the extensional meaning of 'natural' is 'all things'.
2. The intensional meaning of 'categorical' is 'belonging in the categories', and since all things belong in the categories, the extensional meaning of 'categorical' is 'all things'.

Thus, both stems have the same extensional meaning: all things. It follows that what is natural (i.e., all things) is identical with what is categorical (i.e., all things). Therefore, what is supernatural (i.e., outside and above all things) is identical with what is transcategorical (i.e., outside and above all things). Thus, what is supernatural is exactly the same as what is transcategorical. What is supernatural is also unconditionally the same as what is transcategorical, simply because it is outside and above all things and thus not conditional upon any thing. So, the referent of the terms is exactly and unconditionally the same, i.e., identical in the strictest sense of the word.

Notes:
  (a) For what I mean with 'all things', please see the note to section 1.1.1.2.
  (b) Referential equivalents can give meaning to a notion. For example: If someone does not know what 'blattaria' means but is familiar with the term 'cockroaches', then it can be helpful to explain that 'blattaria' means 'cockroaches'. Regardless of whether this qualifies as a proper definition of 'blattaria', it certainly gives meaning to the term 'blattaria'. (Leibniz and others discussed this at length.)

Rationale 2: What has no properties, does not fit in any category.

That God is supernatural, not a thing, means that God has no (real, natural) properties. That God has no properties, means that God does not belong in any particular category, i.e., that God is transcategorical. In other words, that God has no properties, means that no genera-differentiae can be predicated of God, i.e., that God has no (real, categorical) predicates.

Notes:
  (a) I consider properties to be natural/ontological, and predicates to be their categorical/logical counterparts. More on this in chapter 3, 'God is transconceptual'.

What does it mean for God to be transcategorical?

In this section, I will discuss some implications of God being transcategorical.

2.1. God is outside and above the categorical

That God is transcategorical, means that God transcends the categorical, i.e., that God is outside and above the categorical.

2.1.1. God is outside and above all genera-differentiae

That God is transcategorical, outside and above the categorical, means that God is outside and above all genera-differentiae.

2.1.1.1. God is outside and above all predicates

That God is transcategorical, outside and above the categorical, outside and above all genera-differentiae, means that God is outside and above all predicates because all (real) predicates are genera-differentiae.

2.2. God is not categorical

That God is transcategorical, outside and above the categorical, means that God is not categorical.

Notes:
   (a) It seems Aristotle believed that what is transcategorical (i.e., being) is not just outside and above all categories but also pervades all categories.

This seems to be a mistake based on the assumption that things that *appear to be*, *are*. But that things *appear to be*, does not mean that they *are* (i.e., that they also exist in some other way than as an appearance).

2.2.1. No genera-differentiae can be predicated of God

That God is transcategorical, outside and above the categorical, outside and above all genera-differentiae, means that no genera-differentiae can be predicated of God.

Notes:
    (a) You may agree that God has no genera but nevertheless believe that God has differentiae. But that is not possible. A differentia is that which distinguishes some things in a genus from other things in the same genus. So, if God has no genera, God has no differentiae either.

2.2.1.1. No predicates can be predicated of God (i.e., God is predicateless)

That God is transcategorical, outside and above the categorical, outside and above all predicates, means no predicates can be predicated of God. God is predicateless.

Notes:
    (a) That God is predicateless does not mean that God is a thing without predicates, but that God is not a thing.
    (b) 'Predicateless' itself is not a predicate, just like 'colourless' is not a colour. 'Predicateless' is not a (real, categorical) predicate because it is neither a category (i.e., genus), nor can it be said of anything that belongs in the categories (i.e., anything of which genera and differentiae can be predicated). 'Predicateless' is, and only applies to, what transcends the categories (i.e., being, God). Just like supernatural, transcategorical, existence, attributeless, and many others that apply to God. Thus, God can be predicateless and yet supernatural, transcategorical, attributeless, being, and so on.
    (c) To claim that God is predicateless may seem a contradiction-in-terms because it claims that God has the predicate of being without predicates.

But it is not a contradiction-in-terms because 'predicateless' is not a real predicate. More on this in chapter 4.

(d) I am not just claiming that transcategorical notions are not predicates (as Kant did when he said that being is not a (real) predicate, and to which I agree), but also that no (real, categorical) predicates can be predicated of what is transcategorical.

2.3. Anything that is categorical, is not God

That God is transcategorical, outside and above the categorical, not categorical, means that anything that is categorical, is not God.

2.3.1. Anything of which genera-differentiae can be predicated, is not God

That God is transcategorical, outside and above the categorical, not categorical but outside and above all genera-differentiae, so no genera-differentiae can be predicated of God, means that anything of which genera-differentiae can be predicated, is not God.

2.3.1.1. Anything of which predicates can be predicated, is not God

That God is transcategorical, outside and above the categorical, not categorical but outside and above all predicates, so no predicates can be predicated of God, means that anything of which predicates can be predicated, is not God.

2.4. Other implications of God being transcategorical

2.4.1. Categorical and predicate logics cannot deal with God

That God is transcategorical, outside and above the categorical, and thus not categorical, means that categorical logics (e.g., Aristotelian syllogistic logic) cannot accommodate God because categorical logics require their terms to be categorical.

Similarly, if God is transcategorical, outside and above the categorical, and thus predicateless, predicate logics (e.g., first order predicate logic and most other modern logics) cannot deal with God because predicate logics require predicates, i.e., genera–differentiae, categories.

— it does to me

Notes:

(a) This does not mean that we cannot reason about God. We can even reason categorically about God, as long as it is negatively. In Abrahamic religions, this is called (the) *via negativa*, in Hinduism it is known as *neti-neti* (not this, not this). Negating that God fits in any category by denying God each and every predicate. Or we can use 'identity logic' (employing synonyms and referential equivalents) because 'identity' does not require predicates. Perhaps we can even use certain formal logical systems, provided they do not require the terms to be categorical, so they can thus deal with transcategorical notions. The most obvious formal logical system may be sentence logic, aka propositional logic. Last but not least, we can use bare reason. After all, logical systems may offer sets of rules to facilitate good reasoning, but we are not obliged to use them. Especially not where the logical system fails or where it costs more to explain or defend the logical system than it helps in making the argument. Of course, relying on bare reason means we will need to be extra alert, and deal with certain technical issues as they arise.

what is bare reason.

2.4.2. God cannot be defined (categorically)

That God is transcategorical, means God cannot be defined (properly) because proper definitions are categorical (e.g., consist of genera-differentiae). Thus, God has no intensional meaning (i.e., no *Sinn*, 'sense', qualitative identity), and may, strictly speaking, be non-sensical. For example, when we are asked if God is blue or not blue, we cannot say that God is blue, nor can we say that God is not blue, nor can we say that God is both blue and not blue, nor can we say that God is neither blue nor not blue, nor can we say that we do not know. We cannot answer the question because it presupposes that God has a colour, but God does not have any colour at all, God is colourless. The question is invalid. We could say that it makes a 'category mistake'. But that would be an unfortunate expression in this context because the question does not confuse categories (i.e., genera), but confuses all categories with what is outside and above all categories.

Notes:

(a) That God has no intensional meaning, does not mean 'God' has no meaning at all. For example, God has extensional meaning (i.e., *Bedeutung*, 'reference', numerical identity).

Summary of the chapter

If God is supernatural:

2.   God is transcategorical
   - 2.1.   God is outside and above the categorical
     - 2.1.1.   God is outside and above all genera-differentiae
       - 2.1.1.1.   God is outside and above all predicates
   - 2.2.   God is not categorical
     - 2.2.1.   No genera-differentiae can be predicated of God
       - 2.2.1.1.   No predicates can be predicated of God (i.e., God is predicateless)
   - 2.3.   Anything that is categorical, is not God
     - 2.3.1.   Anything of which genera-differentiae can be predicated, is not God
       - 2.3.1.1.   Anything of which predicates can be predicated, is not God
   - 2.4.   Other implications
     - 2.4.1.   Categorical and predicate logics cannot deal with God
     - 2.4.2.   God cannot be defined (categorically)

3. GOD IS TRANSCONCEPTUAL

In this chapter, I will explain what I mean with 'transconceptual', and then show that, given that God is (ontologically speaking) supernatural and (logically speaking) transcategorical, God is (epistemologically speaking) transconceptual, and then discuss some implications of God being transconceptual.

This is step 3 of the philosophical, non-sectarian, 'dry' account of God as supernatural.

The claim that 'God is transconceptual' is the simplified (contrapositive) version of the statement that 'what is not transconceptual, is not what is God'. Thus, it should not be taken to imply that God exists. (In logical terms, it lacks existential import.)

What does 'transconceptual' mean?

'Transconceptual' literally means 'beyond the conceptual'. 'Trans-' comes from Latin *trans*, meaning 'across, beyond, on the other side of', which I consider to be synonymous with 'super-'. 'Conceptual' comes from Latin *concipere*, meaning 'to gather, to conceive'. So, 'conceptual' means 'conceivable', and 'transconceptual' means 'beyond the conceivable'.

Notes:
  (a) A concept consists of a subject-term (e.g., 'human being') and predicates (e.g., 'rational animal'). The subject-term also serves as the name of the concept (i.e., denotes the concept). The predicates consist of genera (and possibly differentiae) that are predicated of the subject-term.

Figure 1: What I mean with 'concept'

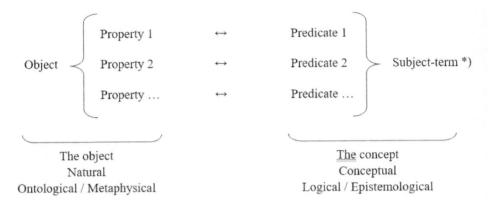

* The subject-term also serves as the name of the concept.

(b) A concept is the (logical-epistemological) counterpart of the (ontological-metaphysical) object; Predicates are the epistemological counterparts of properties. A note to this note: 'Object' is meant in the widest sense of the word, as 'anything that is object', 'anything that appears', 'any phenomenon', regardless of whether it is supposedly physical or mental.

(c) If genera can be predicated of a subject-term, the object that the subject-term denotes is conceptual (i.e., it can be conceptualized, it is conceptualizable, it is conceivable). If no genera can be predicated of a subject-term, the term is not conceptual (i.e., it cannot be conceptualized, is unconceptualizable, it is inconceivable).

(d) In rational discourse, we typically expect the notions (or 'terms') to be defined conceptually (in terms of genera-differentiae) and have conceptual meaning (i.e., genera-differentiae). If notions are not conceptual, they are often considered to be vacuous ('without meaning'), in which case any discourse based on such notions would be meaningless. But the fact that non-conceptual notions cannot be defined conceptually, does not mean that they cannot be defined at all or are meaningless. They may have no conceptual meaning (i.e., intensional, *Sinn*, "sense", qualitative identity), but they can have referential meaning (i.e., extensional, Bedeutung, "reference", numeric identity). They can be identified using synonyms or referential equivalents. Arguably, they can also be defined by pointing them out.

Thus, they can have meaning after all. To summarize the differences between conceptual and transconceptual notions:

Table 1: Conceptual versus transconceptual notions

Conceptual notions	Transconceptual notions
Notions that are conceptualizable, conceivable.	Notions that are not conceptual(izable), inconceivable.
Notions of which genera-differentiae (i.e., categorical, real predicates) can be predicated.	Notions of which no genera-differentiae (i.e., categorical, real predicates) can be predicated.
Notions that have real predicates, i.e., notions that have **attributes**.	Notions that have no real predicates i.e., notions that are **attributeless**.
Notions that refer to things that belong in the categories, things that are **categorical**.	Notions that refer to what does not belong in the categories, what is **transcategorical**.
Notions that refer to **natural objects**.	Notions that refer to the **supernatural subject**.
Notions that have "sense" and may have "reference".	Notions that have no "sense" but may have "reference".
Notions that are comprehensible, comparable.	Notions that are incomprehensible. incomparable.

God is transconceptual

There are different ways to argue for this point.

Rationale 1: No properties, no predicates, no concept.

That God is supernatural, means that God has no (real, natural) properties; That God has no (real, natural) properties, means that God has no (real, categorical) predicates; That God has no (real, categorical) predicates, means that God is not a subject-term of which genera-differentiae can be predicated; That God is not a subject-term of which genera-differentiae can be predicated, means that God is not a concept, not conceptual, cannot be conceptualized, cannot be conceived, but is transconceptual, inconceivable.

Rationale 2: Exactly and unconditionally the same.

Although the notions, transcategorical and transconceptual, may seem to have a different intensional meaning (i.e., 'Sinn', 'sense', qualitative identity), they have the same extensional meaning (i.e., 'Bedeutung', 'reference', numerical identity):
1.   The intensional meaning of 'categorical' is 'belonging in the categories', and since all things belong in the categories, the extensional meaning of 'categorical' is 'all things'.
2.   The intensional meaning of 'conceptual' is 'conceivable, conceptualizable', and since all things can be conceived-conceptualized, the extensional meaning of 'conceptual' is 'all things'. In less technical terms, since all except God can be conceived, the extensional meaning of 'conceptual' is 'all things'.
     Thus, both stems have the same extensional meaning: all things. It follows that what is categorical (i.e., all things) is identical with what is conceptual (i.e., all things). Therefore, what is transcategorical (i.e., outside and above all things) is identical with what is transconceptual (i.e., outside and above all things). Thus, what is transcategorical is exactly the same as what is transconceptual. What is transcategorical is also unconditionally the same as what is transconceptual, simply because it is outside and above all things and is thus not conditional upon anything. So, the referent of the terms is exactly and unconditionally the same, i.e., identical in the strictest sense of the word.

NO, NO

There could be lots of

What does it mean for God to be transconceptual?

In this section, I will discuss some implications of God being transconceptual.

3.1. God is not conceptual, conceivable

That God is transconceptual, means that God is not conceptual, conceivable.

3.1.1. God cannot be conceptualized, conceived

That God is transconceptual, not conceptual, means that God cannot be conceptualized, conceived (i.e., imagined, comprehended, compared).

Notes:
(a) Only attributes can be conceived. In other words, only things that have properties and of which genera-differentiae can be predicated, can be conceived. God does not have attributes, neither properties nor predicates, and thus cannot be conceived.

3.1.2. God is not a concept

That God is transconceptual, means that God is not a subject-term of which genera-differentiae can be predicated, i.e., God is not a concept.

Notes:
(a) Given that concepts require predicates, the idea of a concept without predicates (i.e., without conceptual content) is contradictory. Non-conceptual notions, like 'God' and 'supernatural', do not denote concepts.
(b) If you expect this account of God to yield a concept of God or reveal the nature of God (the qualitative identity, the intensional meaning, or

otherwise list properties, distinguishing features, characteristics, qualities) of God, you are expecting the impossible.

3.1.3. God cannot be defined (conceptually)

That God is transconceptual, predicateless, means that God cannot be defined in the traditional way, conceptually, as a subject-term of which genera-differentiae are predicated.

3.1.4. God cannot be known (conceptually)

That God is transconceptual, means that God cannot be known (conceptually) because only concepts can be known (conceptually).

Notes:
    (a) Only what is conceptual, i.e., what has attributes, can be known. Even if there were things-in-themselves, only their attributes could be known.
    (b) Arguably, there are other, non-conceptual ways of knowing. I am not denying that God can be known in such ways, but merely that God can be known conceptually.

3.1.5. God has no conceptual meaning

That God is transconceptual, not conceptual, means that God has no conceptual meaning, no intensional meaning, no *Sinn*, no 'sense', no qualitative identity.

Notes:
    (a) That God has no intensional meaning does not mean that God has no meaning at all, e.g., extensional, *Bedeutung*, 'reference', numerical identity.

3.1.6. St Anselm's ontological argument does not work

That God is transconceptual, inconceivable, means that St Anselm's ontological argument does not work. The argument depends on the idea that God exists in the mind, i.e., that God is conceivable, but if God is supernatural, God is inconceivable, and the argument does not work.

Summary of the chapter

If God is supernatural and transcategorical:
3.   God is transconceptual.
    3.1.   God is not conceptual, conceivable.
        3.1.1.   God is not a concept.
        3.1.2.   God cannot be conceptualized, conceived.
        3.1.3.   God cannot be defined (conceptually).
        3.1.4.   God cannot be known (conceptually).
        3.1.5.   God has no conceptual meaning.
        3.1.6.   St Anselm's ontological argument does not work.

4. GOD IS ATTRIBUTELESS

In this chapter, I will explain what I mean with 'attributeless', and then show that, given that God is (ontologically speaking) supernatural, (logically speaking) transcategorical, and (epistemologically speaking) transconceptual, God is attributeless, and then discuss some implications of God being attributeless.

This is step 4 of the philosophical, non-sectarian, 'dry' account of God as supernatural.

The claim that 'God is attributeless' is the simplified (contrapositive) version of the statement that 'what is not attributeless, is not what is God'. Thus, it should not be taken to imply that God exists. (In logical terms, it lacks existential import.)

That God is attributeless is a very important point in this account of God. For example: Because it may well be the most profound notion of God, the common root of notions of God like 'supernatural' and 'simple'. Also, because it allows me to prove that there cannot be more than one God, and that God exists.

What does 'attributeless' mean?

'Attributeless' means 'without attributes'. With 'attributes', I mean 'predicates and properties'. With 'predicates' I mean real predicates, i.e., categorical predicates, genera-differentiae, things that give a term intensional meaning, *Sinn*, 'sense', qualitative identity. With 'properties', I mean real properties, i.e., natural properties, distinguishing features, qualities, characteristics, things that some things appear to have but others not. Because it is sometimes hard to distinguish between predicates and properties, and because the distinction is not relevant here, I will use 'attributes' to refer to both. The suffix '-less' means 'without'. Thus, with 'attributeless', I mean 'without predicates and properties'.

Notes:

    (a)   'Attributeless' itself is not an attribute, just like 'colourless' is not a colour. 'Attributeless' itself is not a (real) attribute because 'attributeless' is neither a (real) predicate nor a (real) property.

'Attributeless' is not a (real) predicate because it is not categorical. It is neither a category, nor belongs in the categories, nor can it be said of anything that belongs in the categories. 'Attributeless' is not a (real) property because it is not natural. It is not a feature that distinguishes some things from other things. 'Attributeless' is, and only applies to, what is transcategorical, i.e., supernatural, which is not a thing.

God is attributeless

There are different ways to argue for this point.

Rationale 1: No properties, and thus no predicates, and thus attributeless.

That God is supernatural (i.e., without real properties) and thus transcategorical (i.e., without real predicates), means that God is attributeless (i.e., without real properties and predicates).

In other words: that God is supernatural, means that God is propertyless (see chapter 1) and predicateless (see chapter 2). That God is propertyless and predicateless, means that God is attributeless.

Rationale 2: Exactly and unconditionally the same.

Although the terms, 'transcategorical' and 'attributeless', may seem to have a different intensional meaning (i.e., *Sinn*, 'sense', qualitative identity), they have the exact same extensional meaning (i.e., *Bedeutung*, 'reference', numerical identity). They have the exact same extensional meaning because:
1. what is transcategorical is that which is outside and above all things (because all things belong in the categories) and
2. what is attributeless is that which is outside and above all things (because all things have attributes).
They may even have the same intensional meaning because:
1. to say that something is transcategorical is to say that it does not belong in the categories, that no categorical predicates (i.e., genera-differentiae) can be predicated of it, and thus that it is attributeless.

2. to say that something is attributeless is to say that no categorical predicates can be predicated of it, that it does not belong in the categories, and thus that it is transcategorical.

It follows that what is transcategorical is exactly the same as what is attributeless. What is transcategorical is also unconditionally the same as what is attributeless, simply because it is outside and above all things and is thus not conditional upon anything. So, the referent of the terms is exactly and unconditionally the same, i.e., identical in the strictest sense of the word.

Notes:

    (a) To claim that God is attributeless may seem a contradiction-in-terms because it claims that God has the attribute of being without attributes. But it is not a contradiction-in-terms because 'attributeless' is not a real attribute. Just like 'colorless' is not a real color.

    (b) That God is attributeless may seem to contradict the fact that God has all of the typical attributes of God. But, again, it does not. On the one hand: That God is attributeless means that God has all "attributes" that are referentially equivalent with 'attributeless', e.g., 'transcategorical' and 'transconceptual' (but these are not real attributes). On the other hand: That God is attributeless, means that God *appears to have* all of the typical attributes of God (but God does not really *have* these attributes). They are just different ways or attempts, if ultimately inadequate, of pointing out that that God is attributeless (i.e., limitless in all or some respects).

    (c) That God is attributeless does not mean that God is a thing without attributes (which would be contradictory), but that God is not a thing (and thus has no attributes).

    (d) You may be tempted to object that 'Surely, God is more than just attributeless!'. But this objection is based on a misunderstanding. It is based on the misunderstanding that a God with attributes could be more than a God without attributes. But that is not the case. Only a God without attributes is completely unlimited and thus truly infinite. Thus, there cannot be any God that is more than a God that is attributeless. For more on this, please see the opening pages of Part II.

What does it mean for God to be attributeless?

In this section, I will discuss some implications of God being attributeless.

4.1. God is simple

That God is attributeless, means that God is simple. Absolutely simple. Even simpler than having only one or just a few attributes.

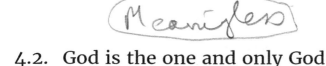

Meaningless

4.2. God is the one and only God

Let me put this in the form of an argument:

[P1]   God is attributeless.

[P2]   Of what is attributeless, there cannot be more than one.

For there to be multiple, they would have to differ. To differ, one must have an attribute that the other lacks. (This is known as the principle of the identity of indiscernibles, usually attributed to Wilhelm Gottfried Leibniz, *Discourse on Metaphysics*, 1686) But what is attributeless, does not have any attributes. Hence, one of what is attributeless cannot differ from another of what is attributeless. Thus, of what is attributeless, there cannot be more than one.

[C]   Therefore, of what is God, there cannot be more than one.

This conclusion can be worded in different ways, for example as 'God is the one and only God'. I will often use 'the one and only' because it is linguistically more convenient, albeit less accurate, than 'not more than one'.

but it is more likely that there is none

Summary of the chapter

If God is supernatural, transcategorical, and transconceptual:
4. God is attributeless.
    4.1. God is simple.
    4.2. God is the one and only God.

Notes to the chapter

When someone says that God has real attributes, it is either because:
(a) (s)he has realized what God is but (s)he feels the truth is too radical and shocking, so (s)he prefers more euphemistic, if perhaps ultimately inadequate, descriptions of God, or
(b) (s)he has realized what God is but (s)he has not found the right words to say it, or
(c) (s)he has not realized what God is (i.e., (s)he is genuinely mistaken).

It is impossible to think of what is attributeless, to conceive what is absolutely simple, to conceptualize what cannot be conceptualized (just like it is impossible to think of what is infinite). The tallest man cannot reach heaven, says Proverbs, and so it is: The greatest we can imagine, is not God because God is greater-than-the-greatest (and less-than-the-least).

It also means that God cannot be imagined. Any image of God is not God. Not just because it is an image of God (and not God itself) but also, and more importantly, because God does not have attributes, and any image of God requires attributing attributes to God. Thus, any image of God (however beautiful or awe-inspiring) is necessarily wrong, blasphemy, sin, ascribing (natural) attributes to what is supernatural. It will be worshipped (like a golden calf). It results in idolatry. That is why the second commandment warns us against making an image of God. No verbal or pictorial border can be drawn around the supernatural. Thus, every image of God is mistaken, misleading.

5. GOD IS EXTRAORDINARY

In this chapter, I will explain what I mean with 'extraordinary', and then show that, given that God is (ontologically speaking) supernatural, (logically speaking) transcategorical, and (epistemologically speaking) transconceptual, God is (colloquially speaking) extraordinary, and then discuss some implications of God being extraordinary.

This is step 5 of the philosophical, non-sectarian, 'dry' account of God as supernatural.

The claim that 'God is extraordinary' is the simplified (contrapositive) version of the statement that 'what is not extraordinary, is not what is God'. Thus, it should not be taken to imply that God exists. (In logical terms, it lacks existential import.)

What does 'extraordinary' mean?

'Extraordinary' literally means 'out of the ordinary'. 'Extra-' comes from Latin *extra-*, meaning 'outside, beyond the scope of', which I consider to be synonymous with 'super-'. 'Ordinary' comes from Latin ordo, meaning 'order', which I take to refer to the usual, common order: In ontological terms, the natural order (of things that are ordered according to the laws of nature); in logical terms, the categorical order (of things that can be ordered into categories); in epistemological terms, the conceptual order (all things that are ordered according to what can be predicated of them, i.e., categorically).

'Extraordinary' is not just used in this literal, strict, absolute sense, but also in a figurative, loose, relative sense. In the absolute sense, 'extra-ordinary' means 'outside and above the ordinary', i.e., 'of a different order', synonymous to, e.g., 'un-usual' and 'exceptio-nal' (in their strict sense). In a relative sense, 'extraordinary' means 'different from ordinary things', i.e., 'different from things within the normal order', synonymous to, e.g., 'special', 'strange', 'odd', and to 'unusual' and 'exceptional' (in their loose sense). Of course, what is extraordinary in the absolute sense, will also appear to be extraordinary in the relative sense.

God is extraordinary

That God is super-natural, outside and above the natural order, means that God is extra-ordinary in the absolute sense (i.e., God is of a different order) and in the relative sense (i.e., God is different from ordinary things). For example, if God is supernatural, God is not subject to the laws of nature (i.e., God is extraordinary in the absolute sense) and thus God appears to defy the laws of nature (i.e., God appears to be extraordinary in the relative sense).

That God is super-natural, means that God is trans-categorical and trans-conceptual, which are just different ways, each in their domain, of saying that God is extra-ordinary. All of the basic terms, 'natural', 'categorical', 'conceptual', and 'ordinary', have the same referent: 'all else', 'all things'. And all of the prefixes, 'super-', 'trans-', and 'extra-', have the same meaning: 'outside and above'. Therefore, to say that God is supernatural, transcategorical, transconceptual, is to say that God is extraordinary (in the absolute sense).

Table 2: God is extraordinary – Out of the natural, categorical, conceptual order

	God	All else
Ontologically speaking	Super–	Natural
Logically speaking	Trans–	Categorical
Epistemologically speaking	Trans–	Conceptual
Colloquially speaking	Extra–	Ordinary

SUMMARY OF CHAPTER 1 TO 5

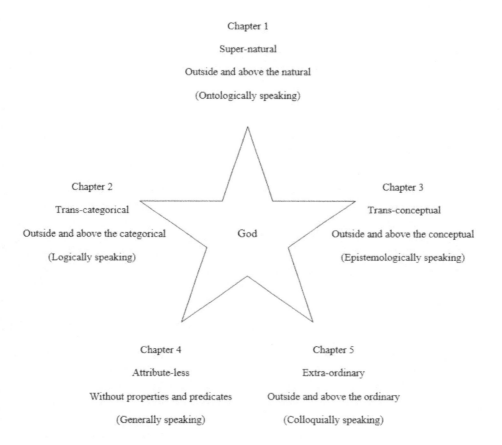

Chapter 1

Super-natural

Outside and above the natural

(Ontologically speaking)

Chapter 2

Trans-categorical

Outside and above the categorical

(Logically speaking)

God

Chapter 3

Trans-conceptual

Outside and above the conceptual

(Epistemologically speaking)

Chapter 4

Attribute-less

Without properties and predicates

(Generally speaking)

Chapter 5

Extra-ordinary

Outside and above the ordinary

(Colloquially speaking)

In the following three sections, I will show that −given that God is supernatural− God is identical (i.e., referentially equivalent) with some of the most familiar notions.

I will then go on to show that −given that God is referentially equivalent with these notions− God *is* (i.e., exists, is real, actual, factual, and not merely apparent), is essential (i.e., indispensable, necessary), and good (i.e., ought to *be*).

6. GOD IS *BEING*

In this chapter, I will explain what I mean with '*being*' or '*being(ness)*', and then show that –given that God is supernatural– God is *being(ness)*.

What does '*being(ness)*' mean?

With '*being*' or '*beingness*', I mean the trivial notion of *being(ness)*, i.e., that which the word '*am*' refers to when I say that 'I *am*'. In more technical terms, *being(ness)* means 'essence' (from Latin *essentia*, from *esse*, meaning '*to be*', used to translate the Greek *ousia*). With 'essense', I mean ' the core, the essential, that which remains when a thing is stripped of all that it *appears to be*, that without which something could not be (identified, defined, categorized as) what it is, or even *be* at all. *Being(ness)* is the essence (i.e. *being*) of myself and of all else. Thus, *being(ness)* is at once individual and universal:

- Individual in the sense that *being(ness)* is my essence (i.e. *being*). In this sense, *being(ness)* can be called the self, soul, spirit, psyche, presence, or awareness (all in the purest, thinnest, least weighty sense of the words). It is that which remains when I am stripped of all that I appear to be; that without which I could not be what I am, or even *be* at all.
- Universal in the sense that *being(ness)* is the essence (i.e. *being*) of all else, of all that *appears to me*, of the universe. It is that which remains when all else is stripped of all that it appears to be. It is that without which all else could be what it is, or even *(appear to) be* at all.

Notes:
 (a) '*Being(ness)*' cannot be defined in the traditional way (i.e., categorically), in terms of the categories it belongs to (i.e., genera) and what distinguishes it from other things in those categories (i.e., differentiae). *) '*Being(ness)*' cannot be defined categorically because *being(ness)* does not belong in any particular categories. *Being(ness)* transcends the categories, is transcategorical, and thus attributeless

(i.e., propertyless and predicateless, without distinguishing features). Because *being(ness)* is transcategorical and attributeless, *being(ness)* is transconceptual (i.e., not a subject-term of which genera-differentiae can be predicated), not a concept, not conceptual, cannot be conceived, and has no conceptual meaning, i.e., no intensional meaning, *Sinn*, 'sense', qualitative identity.

*) Arguably, *being(ness)* can be defined categorically but only negatively (i.e., *via negativa, neti-neti*), all-exclusively (i.e., by denying *being(ness)* each and every genera-differentiae, or all-inclusively (by predicating all genera (and differentiae) of it). I say, arguably, because these ways still fail to give '*being(ness)*' any real, conceptual meaning, which requires real, categorical predicates, i.e., genera-differentiae. To define notions all-inclusively (e.g., in terms of the omni-"attributes") or all-exclusively (e.g., in terms of the in-/un-/-less-"attributes", e.g., infinite, limitless, unlimited) is to deny them having any particular genera-differentiae. Such "definitions" are just ways or attempts to explain the non-conceptual notion in conceptual terms, which cannot yield a proper, satisfactory definition.

(b) If the meaning of '*being(ness)*' seems elusive, that is just because *being(ness)* is transconceptual and thus cannot be analyzed and thought (about) in the usual (conceptual) way in which we think about (the genera-differentiae of) natural things.

(c) '*Being(ness)*' is neither a noun (referring to, e.g., a thing, an entity, an event) nor a verb (referring to, e.g., a functioning, a happening, an act(ing)). But grammar obliges me to use it as a noun or a verb. So, I use it interchangeably as noun and verb, in order to avoid fixating on either. If it sounds vague to claim that '*being(ness)*' is neither a verb nor a noun, please consider the following analogy: Within the dream, (the) dreaming (of the dream) is neither a thing nor a functioning, right? But if one person in the dream wants to speak with another person in the dream about (the) dreaming (of the dream), he/she has to use '(the) dreaming' as a noun or verb. Likewise, within waking life, (the) *being(ness)* (of the waking life) is neither a thing nor a functioning, right? But if one person in waking life wants to speak with another person in waking life about (the) *being(ness)* (of waking life), he/she has to use '(the) *being(ness)*' as a noun or verb.

(d) '*Being(ness)*' does not refer to a being (e.g. a human being, a supreme being) or beings (e.g., human beings, things). '*Being(ness)*' does not refer to things, neither to anything in particular, nor to merely everything. Instead, '*being(ness)*' refers to the *being(ness)* that all things appear to have (and which does not belong to those things, but to *being(ness)* itself). In other words, '*being(ness)*' can provisionally be taken to refer to 'existence' and 'existing', but certainly not to any existent(s). *Being(ness)* is not a thing.

(e) '*Being(ness)*' refers to *being(ness)* as such, in and of and by itself, *being(ness)* qua *being(ness)*, as explained by Aristotle in the opening pages of Book E of his First Philosophy –a work that has confusingly become known as Metaphysics. Confusingly, because *being(ness)* qua *being(ness)* is not just meta-physical but also meta-mental.

God = being(ness)

Being(ness) is neither red nor blue, neither big nor small, neither friendly nor unfriendly, in short, *being(ness)* has no distinguishing features, no properties, no predicates, i.e.:

[1]   *Being(ness)* is attributeless.

This will not come as a surprise, at least not to philosophers: Aristotle already famously argued that *being(ness)* transcends the categories and is thus attributeless. And Kant famously argued that *being(ness)* is not a real predicate, not categorical, which approaches the issue from the other side but amounts to the same.

Now, as shown in chapter 4, given that God is supernatural:

[2]   God is attributeless.

Also shown in chapter 4:

[3]   Of what is attributeless, there cannot be more than one.

From [1] and [2] and [3], it follows that:

[4]   God = *being(ness)*.

Being(ness) is attributeless; and God is attributeless; and of what is attributeless, there cannot be more than one; therefore, *being(ness)* is referentially equivalent (i.e., exactly and unconditionally (numerically) identical) with God.

This is Nonsense

7. GOD IS CONSCIOUSNESS

In this chapter, I will explain what I mean with 'consciousness', and then show that –given that God is supernatural– God is consciousness.

What does 'consciousness' mean?

With 'consciousness', I mean 'what is conscious' or, if you consider that to be circular, 'what is aware' or 'that which all else appears to' or 'the subject'.

Notes:
- (a) 'Consciousness' cannot be defined in the traditional way (i.e., categorically, conceptually) and may thus seem elusive. See the notes under 'What does *being(ness)* mean?', reading 'consciousness' instead of '*being(ness)*'.
- (b) If the notion of consciousness seems elusive, that is because, just like *being(ness)*, consciousness has no distinguishing features (i.e., is neither red nor blue, neither big nor small, neither friendly nor unfriendly), has neither (real, natural) properties nor (real, categorical) predicates. Thus, consciousness is not conceptual (i.e., not a subject-term of which genera-differentiae can be predicated), cannot be conceptualized, conceived, analyzed, or thought (about) in the usual (conceptual) way in which we can think about (the attributes of) natural things.
- (c) 'Subject' is to be understood in the thinnest, least weighty sense of the word. Notions like 'the perceiver' and 'the knower' imply too much of an active role for consciousness. Notions like 'the witness' or 'the observer' are slightly better but still seem to imply more than there is to consciousness.
- (d) In the ultimate analysis, consciousness is what I *am*, in essence. I am not something else (i.e., other than consciousness itself, e.g., a human being, a body and/or mind) that *has* consciousness. I can *be* (or, at least, imagine myself to *be*) without body and mind, but I cannot *be* (or even

imagine myself to *be*) without consciousness. In other words, consciousness does not require a host. Consciousness is not (a (mental) state or quality of) something else that happens to be conscious; consciousness is that which is conscious.

God = consciousness

Consciousness is neither red nor blue, neither big nor small, neither friendly nor unfriendly, in short, consciousness has no distinguishing features, no properties, no predicates, i.e.:

[1]   Consciousness is attributeless.

Now, as shown in chapter 4, given that God is supernatural:

[2]   God is attributeless.

Also shown in chapter 4:

[3]   Of what is attributeless, there cannot be more than one.

From [1] and [2] and [3], it follows that:

[4]   God = consciousness.

Consciousness is attributeless; and God is attributeless; and of what is attributeless, there cannot be more than one; therefore, consciousness is referentially equivalent (i.e., exactly and unconditionally (numerically) identical) with God.

Now it seems that GOD is being and GOD is consciousness. They are all the same thing. is he anything else

49

8. GOD IS WHAT I AM

In this chapter, I will explain what I mean with 'what I am', and then show that – given that God is supernatural– God is what I am.

What does 'what I am' mean?

With 'what I am', I mean that which all else appears to.

Notes:
- (a) 'What I am' refers to what I am in essence, that without which I could not be what I am, or even *be* at all, i.e., that which remains when I (mentally) strip myself of all that I am not, of all that is inessential. In other words, 'what I am' refers to that which all else appears to (call it consciousness, the subject, my *being*). 'What I am' refers to the bare self (i.e., barren of any identification with what it is not), to the pure subject (i.e., purified of any identification with what is object to it). 'What I am' refers to that which all else appears to, not to anything that appears to it.
- (b) 'What I am' should not be taken to refer to the person, the human being, the living organism, the body, mind, or any role or function(ing) thereof. Of course, we usually think of ourselves as a person, a human being (e.g., when I say 'Hello, I am Ruud'), with the body (e.g., when I say that 'I am tall'), with the mind (e.g., when I say that 'I am sensitive'), with a role (e.g., when I say that 'I am a professor'), with a function(ing) (e.g., when I say that 'I am thinking' or 'I am feeling good'), and so on. I realize that it is unusual to deny such identifications. But I also realize it is necessary, not only to find God or to make progress in theology and in the philosophy of religion, but also to make progress in philosophy and life in general. So, let me explain why I believe that I cannot be the body, mind, or any role or function(ing) thereof:

a. If I were the body, I would change if the body changed, but I do not. For example: If I cut my nails or hair, it does not change what I am. Even if I lose an arm or a leg, it does not change what I am in essence. The 'I' that believes it had an arm, and now believes it does not have it anymore, is obviously still the same 'I'. Even if I lose my brain, it does not change what I am, at least not if we are to believe the mounting evidence of so-called near-death experiences, where the brain is dead yet the 'I' remains intact (and even continues to perceive, remember, etc. without making use of the sense faculties of the body).

[handwritten: Bad stuff]

b. If I were a (set of) thought(s), feeling(s), or perception(s), I would change if those thoughts, feelings, or perceptions changed, but I do not. For example: If I thought it was going to rain, but now I think it is not, it does not change what I am. If I felt sad yesterday, but I am joyous now, 'I' am still the same 'I'. *[handwritten: No you are not.]*

c. Similarly, if I were some role(s) or function(ing)(s) of the human being, I would change if such role(s) or function(ing)(s) changed, but I do not. If I lose a job, it does not change what I am in essence. The 'I' that believed it had a job and now believes it does not have a job anymore, is obviously still the same 'I'.

(c) The 'I' in 'what I am' is meant token-reflexively. I assume that you can say the same for yourself, e.g., that 'God is what I am'.

(d) 'What I am' (or 'I', 'me', 'myself', and even objectivized as 'the self') cannot be defined in the traditional way (i.e., categorically, conceptually) and may thus seem elusive. For more on this, please see the notes under 'What does *being(ness)* mean?', reading 'what I am' instead of '*being(ness)*'.

God = what I am

What I am, i.e., that which all else appears to, is neither red nor blue, neither big nor small, neither friendly nor unfriendly, in short, what I am has no distinguishing features, no properties, no predicates, i.e.:

what you are is only their thing

[1]   What I am is attributeless.

Everything that appears (to me) has attributes. In fact, it may well be that things are nothing but (a bundle of) attributes. After all, what remains of a thing when it is stripped of all attributes, i.e., of all that it appears to be? Either way: To appear, is to have attributes, and to have attributes, is to appear (if only as a concept). But I am that which all else appears to. So, I cannot appear (to myself). Therefore, I am attributeless (to myself).

why not

Notes:
- (a) The apparent restriction '(to myself)' is not really a restriction. The private claim is, for all means and purposes, universal because I can only ever be conscious of what appears to myself.

Now, as shown in chapter 4, given that God is supernatural:

[2]   God is attributeless.

Also shown in chapter 4:

[3]   Of what is attributeless, there cannot be more than one.

From [1] and [2] and [3], it follows that:

[4]   God = what I am.

What I am is attributeless; and God is attributeless; and of what is attributeless, there cannot be more than one; therefore, what I am is referentially equivalent (i.e., exactly and unconditionally (numerically) identical) with God.

Notes:
- (a) Of course, that 'God = what I am' is a euphemistic way of saying that 'I am God' (i.e., token-reflexively). It surprises me that so many (theistic)

people consider it blasphemous to say that 'I am God'. It surprises me because theistic scriptures often confirm clearly and explicitly that I am God. Especially in Hindu scriptures. For example, in the Mahavakyas (great sayings), *ayam ātmā brahma* (meaning 'I = God'), *aham brahmāsmi* (meaning, 'I am God'). But also in Abrahamic religions. For example, in Exodus 3:14, where God says we should call God 'I am that I am', and if we do as God says, and call God by this name, it points back to ourselves. For example, in prayer, we would say, 'Dear I am that I am, please have mercy'. (It is the perfect mantra!) And in Psalm 86, where God says 'Ye are Gods', and in John 10:30, where Jesus identifies himself with God (and is subsequently accused of blasphemy and threatened, as is happening to me.)

(b) Realizing that 'God is what I am' is variously referred to as apotheosis (from Greek *apo-* 'to change (into), to become' and *theos*, 'God') and divine union (i.e., union with the divine). Both terms are a bit unfortunate, as they suggest that we need to become something else, respectively that we are something else that needs to unite itself with God, while we already are and always already were God. We just (mistakenly) imagined ourselves to be human beings. It was a simple case of mistaken identity.

If I am God then I am supernatural

SUMMARY OF CHAPTER 1 TO 8

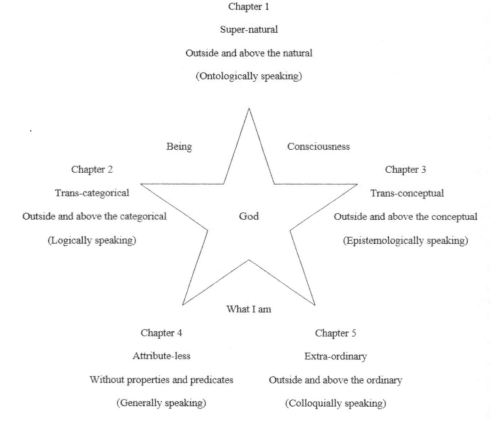

Chapter 1

Super-natural

Outside and above the natural

(Ontologically speaking)

Being

Chapter 2

Trans-categorical

Outside and above the categorical

(Logically speaking)

Consciousness

Chapter 3

Trans-conceptual

Outside and above the conceptual

(Epistemologically speaking)

God

What I am

Chapter 4

Attribute-less

Without properties and predicates

(Generally speaking)

Chapter 5

Extra-ordinary

Outside and above the ordinary

(Colloquially speaking)

In the following four sections, I will show that –given that God is supernatural and referentially equivalent with some of the most familiar notions of the previous chapters– God *is* (i.e., exists, is real, actual, factual, and not merely apparent), and is essential (i.e., indispensable, necessary), and good (i.e., ought to *be*, is necessary).

9. GOD *IS* (I.E., EXISTS, IS REAL, IS WHAT *IS*)

In this chapter, I will explain what I mean with '*is*', and then show that –given that God is supernatural– God *is.* If you are particularly interested in the existence of God, you may also want to see *A natural proof for the existence of God as supernatural* (Ruud Schuurman, 2018).

What does '*is*' mean?

'*Is*' (italicized) is a conjugation of the (existential, intransitive, main) verb '*to be*'. With '*to be*', I mean 'to exist, to be real'. With 'to exist' and 'to be real', I mean 'to be actual, factual, not possibly merely apparent'. With 'actual', I mean 'here and now'. With 'factual', I mean 'in fact, verifiable in experience'. With 'not possibly merely apparent', I mean 'existing in some other way than as a mere appearance'.

Notes:
    (a) The verb 'to be', and conjugations and substantiations thereof, can cause confusion. For example, because:
-    It can be used as an existential, intransitive, main verb, but also, e.g., predicatively, as a transitive verb, and as an auxiliary verb.
-    It is highly irregular and its conjugations (e.g. 'am', 'is', 'are', 'be', 'being', 'was', 'were', 'been', 'will be', etc.) need not readily be recognized as conjugations of the same verb.
-    The word 'being' can be a conjugation (i.e. verb) or substantiation (i.e. noun).

    Subsequently, it may seem that 'to be' is used in many different ways (following Aristotle). I suspect it is not, but that it is often mis-applied. For example, when it is said that things *are*, even though they only *appear to be*. And when it is said that some things *are* blue, even though they only *appear to be* blue.

(b) Where I italicize the verb '*to be*', including conjugations and substantiations thereof, it is used as an existential, intransitive, main verb, synonymous with 'to exist' and 'to be real'.

(c) I use the verb 'to exist', including conjugations and substantiations thereof, in the contemporary sense of '*to be*' and 'to be real'. I do not use 'to exist' in the etymological sense of 'to stand forth, appear out of, emerge, become' (from Latin *existere* or *exsistere*, from *ex*- 'forth, out' and *sistere* 'to cause to stand, take a stand'). In the etymological sense, 'to exist' does not mean 'to be real', but rather 'to be unreal'. It is the very opposite of what it means today. (Latin used different words for '*to be*' (*esse*, which is closer to the contemporary meaning of 'existing') and 'to exist' (*existere* or *exsistere*, which closer to the etymological meaning of 'existing'). Some languages still do. For example, Spanish uses *ser* for '*to be*' (for an enduring fact, absolute) and *estar* for 'to exist' (for a state of affairs, relative). The difference is interesting because things that are thought to exist, possibly merely *appear to be* (i.e., stand forth, also related to the word 'object') and need not *be*, need not exist in some other way than as a mere appearance.

(d) When I say that 'God *is*', I do not mean that 'the 3-letter-word *is*', or that 'the concept *is*', but that 'the referent *is*'. (With 'the referent', I mean that which the word refers to.) In other words, to say of a word that it *is* (i.e., exists, is real), is to say that the referent of the word *is* (i.e., exists, is real).

I will now present three arguments to prove that −given that God is supernatural− God *is* (i.e., exists, is real, actual, factual, and not possibly merely apparent).

Argument 1 (From *being(ness)*)

It seems quite obvious that:

[P1]   Being(ness) is.

There are different ways to argue for this point. Here are some:

Rationale 1: I *am*, therefore *being(ness) is*.

Rationale 2: That *being(ness) is*, is self-evident, undeniable (i.e., necessarily true, analytic). It is metaphysically undeniable, because I would have to *be* to be able to deny that *being(ness) is*. And it is logically undeniable, because to say that '*being(ness) is* not', is a contradiction in terms. To say that *being(ness) is*, is to say that what *is, is*, (i.e., that what is real, is real); to deny it, is to say that what *is, is* not, or that what is not, is (i.e., that what is real, is not real, or that what is not real, is real), which is the very definition of falsity.

Rationale 3: *Being(ness) is* because *being(ness)* is real, that is, actual (i.e., here and now, universally here and eternally now), factual (i.e., in fact, directly verifiable in my own experience, and without use of the senses), and not possibly merely apparent (because *being(ness)* does not appear at all; it is that which all else appears to).

Notes:
- (a) As a reminder: First-person claims, like 'I *am*', are meant token-reflexively, i.e., assuming you can say the same for yourself.
- (b) By claiming that *being(ness) is*, I may seem to commit the fallacy known as 'reification' (meaning 'making into a thing', from Latin *re*, from *res*, meaning 'thing', and *-fy*, meaning 'making into').

    This fallacy occurs when one abstracts a property from the things that exemplify it (or in which it is repeated) and then takes that property to exist in itself, independently of the things that exemplify it. In other words, when one mistakes what is abstract to be concrete.

    To explain the underlying theory: A tomato is red, blood is red, Marilyn Monroe's lips are red, the upper traffic-light is red. These things (e.g., tomatoes, blood) exemplify red(ness). But we can also think-talk about red(ness) as such, without thinking-talking about tomatoes, blood, or any other things that exemplify red(ness). For example, when we think-talk about the wavelengths or frequencies that constitute red(ness). Thus, red(ness) as such can be abstracted from the things that exemplify red(ness). The fallacy of reification occurs when one subsequently considers red(ness) to exist independently of the things that it is abstracted from.

According to some people, this is the fallacy I am committing here. They typically reason as follows: "A tomato *is*, blood *is*, Marilyn Monroe *is*, the traffic-light *is*. These things (e.g., tomatoes, blood) exemplify *being(ness)*. But we can also think-talk about *being(ness)* as such, without thinking-talking about tomatoes, blood, or any other things that exemplify *being(ness)*. For example, when we think-talk about whether *being(ness)* is referentially equivalent with consciousness. Thus, *being(ness)* as such, can be abstracted from the things that exemplify *being(ness)*. The fallacy of reification occurs when you subsequently consider the property of *being(ness)* to exist independently of the things it is abstracted from."

But this reasoning does not apply to *being(ness)*. Because *being(ness)* is not a property. *Being(ness)* is not a distinguishing feature, not a (real) property. *Being(ness)* does not have a frequency or wavelength or any property like that. We cannot think-talk about *being(ness)* in the usual way, i.e., categorically, conceptually. Kant famously explained this. As did Aristotle, albeit indirectly, by explaining that *being(ness)* transcends the categories. Since *being(ness)* is not a property, it cannot be reified. In other words, *being(ness)* is not exemplified in things and thus cannot be abstracted from those things. *Being(ness)* is not exemplified in things because things **are** not, but only **appear to be**. For example: Tomatoes **are** not, but only **appear to be**.

If the difference between '*being*' and '*appearing to be*' seems marginal, please note it is crucial. To fail to notice the difference between what *is* and what *appears to be*, is to commit the fallacy that I call 'The Grand Reification'. That is, to assume that, because a thing appears, it must also exist in some other way than as an appearance. To assume that appearances must be caused by things that exists in themselves. To assume that appearances must be perceptions, representations, after-images of, or otherwise caused by an objective reality. To put it more precisely, it is to assume that, because an appearance appears, it must be caused by something that exist in some other way than as a mere appearance. This is clearly an invalid inference: It infers an objective reality from subjective appearances, which are completely different orders. Also, dreams and hallucinations constitute clear and common counterexamples, showing that appearances need not be perceptions, representations, after images, or otherwise caused by objectively real things.

In summary, *being(ness)* is not a property, things do not exemplify it, therefore this is not a case of reification.

If you agree that:

[P1]   *Being(ness) is.*

and that, as shown in chapter 6:

[P2]   God = *being(ness).*

it follows that:

[C]   God *is.*

The conclusion follows from the premises by the inference known as the substitution of logical equivalents, which is generally considered to be valid. If you agree that the inference is valid, and the premises are true, then so is the conclusion.

Argument 2 (From consciousness)

It seems quite obvious that:

[P1]   Consciousness *is.*

There are different ways to argue for this point. Here are some:

Rationale 1: I am conscious, therefore consciousness *is.*

Rationale 2: That consciousness *is*, is undeniable. It is undeniable because I would have to be conscious to be able to deny that consciousness *is.*

Rationale 3: Consciousness *is* because consciousness is real: actual (i.e., here and now, universally here and eternally now), factual (i.e., in fact, directly verifiable in my own experience, and without use of the senses), and not possibly merely apparent (because consciousness does not appear at all; it is that which all else appears to).

Notes:

(a) By claiming that consciousness *is*, I may seem to commit the fallacy of 'reification', reasoning as follows: "I am conscious, my friend is conscious, the shoemaker is conscious. Thus, consciousness is a property that can be abstracted from the things that exemplify consciousness. The fallacy of 'reification' occurs when you subsequently consider the property of consciousness to exist independently of the things it is abstracted from." But this reasoning does not apply to consciousness. It does not because consciousness is not a property. First of all, because consciousness is not a distinguishing feature. Second, because consciousness is not exemplified in things and thus cannot be abstracted from those things. Things are not conscious (of me); I am conscious (of all things).

If you agree that:

[P1]   Consciousness *is*.

and that, as shown in chapter 7:

[P2]   God = consciousness.

it follows that:

[C]   God *is*.

If you agree that the inference is valid, and the premises are true, then so is the conclusion.

Argument 3 (From what I am)

It seems quite obvious that:

[P1]   What I am, *is*.

There are different ways to argue for this point. Here are some:

Rationale 1: It is undeniable. To say that 'what I am, is not', is to utter a contradiction. What I am has to *be* in order to for me to be able deny that it *is*.

Rationale 2: What I am, *is*, because what I am, is real: actual (i.e., here and now, universally here and eternally now), factual (i.e., in fact, directly verifiable in my own experience, and without use of the senses), and not possibly merely apparent (because what I am, in the ultimate analysis, does not appear at all; what I am, is that which all else appears to).

Rationale 3: Appearances appear to me, therefore I *am*, i.e., what I am, *is*.

Notes:
  (a) That a thing appears to me, does not prove that the thing *is* (i.e., exists in some other way than as an appearance). But the fact that something appears to me, even if it is just an appearance, does prove that I *am* for it to appear to. Let me address each half of the two claims separately:
  -    That a thing appears to me, does not prove that the thing also exists in some other way than as an appearance because appearances can very well appear without such things, for example in a dream. In other words, appearances need not be perceptions, representations, after-images of, or otherwise caused by things that exist in some other way than as an appearance (i.e., real things, things that exist in themselves, an underlying, objective reality). The supposed existence of things in themselves is illicitly inferred from the fact that appearances appear. (I call this 'The Grand Reification'.)
  -    That a thing appears to me, does prove that I *am* for it to appear to. Without me, it could not appear to me.
  (b) By claiming that what I am *is*, I could be considered to commit the fallacy known as 'reification'. My body is what I am (as implied by saying that I am tall, that I am 20 years old, that I am running, and so

on). My mind is what I am (as implied by saying that I am smart, that I am sensitive, and so on). Certain roles I have, are what I am (as implied by saying that I am a husband, a father, a football coach, a carpenter, and so on). Thus, 'what I am' seems to be a universal property that can be abstracted from the things that exemplify what I am. (This may be what Hume called a "bundle".) I can be considered to commit the fallacy of 'reification' when I consider the property of 'what I am' to exist independently of the things that it is abstracted from. But this reasoning does not apply to what I am. It does not because what I am is not a property. First of all, because what I am is not a distinguishing feature. Second, because what I am is not exemplified in things and thus cannot be abstracted from those things.

If you agree that:

[P1]   What I am, *is*.

and that, as shown in chapter 8:

[P2]   God = what I am.

it follows that:

[C]   God *is*.

If you agree that the inference is valid, and the premises are true, then so is the conclusion.

10. GOD IS ESSENTIAL (I.E., THE ESSENCE, WHAT IS ESSENTIAL)

In this chapter, I will explain what I mean with 'essential', and then show that – given that God is supernatural– God is essential.

What does 'essential' mean?

With 'essential', I mean 'indispensable, necessary'. X is essential to Y, if Y could not be Y (and/or not *be* at all) without X. In other words, if Y is stripped of everything that it can do without (i.e., all that is not essential, not X), what remains (i.e., what is essential, X) is that which is essential to Y (i.e., is Y).

Argument 1 (From *being(ness)*)

It seems quite obvious that:

[P1]   *Being(ness)* is essential (i.e., indispensable, necessary).

There are different ways to argue for this point. Here are some:

Rationale 1: *Being(ness)* is essential to me because I could not *be* without *being(ness)*. *Being(ness)* is the essence (i.e., *being(ness)*) of myself.

Rationale 2: *Being(ness)* is essential to all else because all else could not *be*, or even *appear to be*, without *being(ness)*. *Being(ness)* is the essence (i.e., *being(ness)*) of all else.

Rationale 3: *Being(ness)* is essential because *being(ness)* literally means essence (from Latin *esse*, meaning 'to be').

If you agree that:

[P1]   *Being(ness)* is essential (i.e., indispensable, necessary).

and that, as we have seen in chapter 6:

[P2]   God = *being(ness)*.

it follows that:

[C]   God is essential (i.e., indispensable, necessary).

If you agree that the inference is valid, and the premises are true, then so is the conclusion.

Argument 2 (From consciousness)

It seems quite obvious that:

[P1]   Consciousness is essential (i.e., indispensable, necessary).

There are different ways to argue for this point. Here are some:

Rationale 1: Consciousness is essential because without consciousness, I could not be conscious of anything, I could not know anything, not even that I am. Without consciousness, I could not *be* (or, at least, I could not know that I *am*, which amounts to the same. Effectively, *to be* = *to be conscious*). Thus, consciousness is literally essential.

Rationale 2: Consciousness is essential because without consciousness I could not be what I am, or even *be* at all. In the ultimate analysis, I am consciousness (having a human experience) rather than a human being (having a conscious experience). I am not something else that *has* consciousness; I *am* consciousness.

If you agree that:

[P1]   Consciousness is essential (i.e., indispensable, necessary).

and that, as we have seen in chapter 7:

[P2]   God = consciousness.

it follows that:

[C]   God is essential (i.e., indispensable, necessary).

If you agree that the inference is valid, and the premises are true, then so is the conclusion.

Argument 3 (From what I am)

It seems quite obvious that:

[P1]   What I am, is essential (i.e., indispensable, necessary).

Rationale: What I am, is essential because without what I am, I could not be what I am, or *be* at all. Moreover, without what I am, nothing could appear to me, so what I am is essential to all else.

If you agree that:

[P1]   What I am, is essential (i.e., indispensable, necessary).

and that, as shown in chapter 8:

[P2]   God = what I am.

Then it follows that:

[C]   God is essential (i.e., indispensable, necessary).

If you agree that the inference is valid, and the premises are true, then so is the conclusion.

11. GOD IS GOOD (I.E., WHAT IS GOOD, WHAT OUGHT TO BE)

In this chapter, I will explain what I mean with 'good', and then show that –given that God is supernatural– God is good.

What does 'good' mean?

With 'what is good' I mean 'what ought to *be*'. With 'what ought to *be*', I mean 'what *is* necessarily, inevitably'.

Argument 1 (from what *is*)

[1]   God (is what) *is*. (See chapter 9.)
[2]   What *is*, is what ought to *be*. *)
[3]   What ought to *be*, (is what) is good.
[4]   Therefore, God (is what) is good.

Notes:
   *)   Relatively speaking: Considering all that *was* and all that *will be*, what *is*, is what ought to *be*. (This solves Hume's is/ought problem, I presume.) Absolutely speaking: What *is*, is what ought to *be*, just because it *is*. (Another way to solve the is/ought problem.) Hence, looking through the eyes of God, all is indeed good, always and everywhere. After all, every imagined point in the future *is*, here and now by the time the future becomes present, here and now, if the imagined future does indeed become present at all. In other words: Only what *is*, here and now, *is*; All else only *appears to be*, there and then. All else (e.g., past and

future, the universe) is inferred from what *is*, here and now. The point of origin (of time, space, and causality), the first uncaused cause is not in the past (nor in the future), but *is*, here and now. After all, else is inferred from and contingent upon what *is*, here and now. The fact that something *is*, here and now, allows us to infer its causes somewhere in the past and its effects somewhere in the future. For example: That the forest is on fire, here and now, allows us to infer that it must have been ignited somewhere (at the tallest tree), in the past (an hour ago when the lightning hit), and that it will burn on until it stops somewhere (when it reaches the river), in the future (tomorrow morning).

If you agree that the inference is valid, and the premises are true, then so is the conclusion.

Argument 2 (from what is essential)

[1]   God is essential. (See chapter 10.)
[2]   What is essential is necessary.
[3]   What is necessary, is what ought to *be*.
[4]   What ought to *be*, is good.
[5]   Therefore, God is good.

If you agree that the inference is valid, and the premises are true, then so is the conclusion.

PART II

IS IT STILL
AN ACCOUNT
OF GOD?

This account of God may be based on the credible notion that God is supernatural, and the rest of the account may follow from that basic notion, but is it still an account of God? Is this still an account of the God of Abraham, of the Godhead of the Vedas, of the Unconditioned of the Buddha, and of the Tao of Lao Tzu?

At first sight, some of the conclusions in Part I may seem incompatible with the common notion of God. Especially with the implication that God is attributeless, which seems incompatible with the fact that God has all kinds of attributes. But is it really incompatible? Is the fact that God is supernatural and thus attributeless incompatible with the fact that God appears to have all kinds of attributes? In this chapter, I will show that it is not incompatible. In fact, I will argue that God appears to have all of the typical attributes of God, just because God is supernatural, and thus attributeless. So, this is indeed an account of the one and only God.

I will first give a general, theoretical explanation of how God can be attributeless, and of how God can be attributeless yet appear to have all of the typical "attributes" of God. I will then go on to give specific, practical examples. That is, I will show how around 50 of the typical "attributes" of God follow from the notion of God as supernatural, i.e., attributeless.

A general, theoretical explanation

In this section, I will argue that only a supernatural and thus attributeless God truly qualifies as God. I will also show that, given that God is supernatural and thus attributeless, the typical "attributes" of God nevertheless apply.

"Surely, God is more than just attributeless!"

As we have seen, given that God is supernatural, God is attributeless. But this seems to reduce God to an empty abstraction, a mere nothingness. It seems that what we end up with, is not really God at all. As a friend exclaimed, "Surely, God is more than just attributeless!"

But how could that be true? After all, what is attributeless (and *only* what is attributeless) is really unlimited, limitless, and infinite, truly greater-than-the-greatest, supreme, and so on. After all, to have attributes is to be limited. Attributes limit, negate, distinguish something from what it is not. *Omnis determinatio est negatio* ('all determination is negation') as the scholastics put it. It follows that only what is attributeless, is limitless, unlimited, infinite. Thus, there cannot possibly be anything that is more than "just" attributeless. It follows that God cannot possibly be more than just attributeless.

So, if we try to see God as more than just attributeless, by attributing attributes to God, however noble the attributes may be, we thereby limit God (or, our notion of God). In other words, by forming unto ourselves an image (e.g., a mental image, a concept) of God, however subtle, we thereby inevitably reduce God.

But it is not nearly as bad as it seems. Most of what is said of the God of Abraham and of the godhead of the Vedas, can also be said of a God that is supernatural and thus attributeless. All of the typical attributes of God are ways or attempts, if ultimately inadequate, to say that God is supernatural. Let me explain.

(1) God has all supernatural "attributes"

If God is supernatural, God *has* all *supernatural* "attributes". The supernatural "attributes" are really just different ways of saying that God is supernatural. So, if God is supernatural, God is also transcategorical, transconceptual, attributeless, and extraordinary; God is being(ness), consciousness, and what I am; God is infinite, greater-than-the-greatest, supreme; and so on. All supernatural "attributes" are referentially equivalent (and arguably synonymous) with 'supernatural', and with each other, because, as we have seen, of what is supernatural, there cannot be more than one. Thus, all supernatural "attributes" can be truly attributed to God.

However, as we have seen, the supernatural attributes are not *real* attributes (i.e., neither natural properties, nor categorical predicates).

To summarize this point: If God is supernatural, God has all supernatural "attributes" (i.e., all supernatural "attributes" can be truly attributed to God), but they are not *real* attributes. Thus, they leave God attributeless.

(2) God *appears to have* real attributes

If God is supernatural, God will *appear to have* all of the typical *real* attributes of God. For example: If God is supernatural, God is attributeless, God has no attributes, and thus also no temporal attributes, no beginning or end, and what has no beginning and end, will *appear to be* eternal (i.e., infinitely extended in time), therefore, God will *appear to be* eternal. In this way, most, if not all, of the real attributes that God appears to have, follow from the fact that God is supernatural. God *appears to have* these real attributes just because God is supernatural. They are attempts to say that God is supernatural. They describe how God appears to us when we look at God through the eyes of man. They are ways or attempts (if ultimately inadequate) of pointing out that God is supernatural.

The real attributes are real in the sense that they are natural properties and/or categorical predicates.

However, unless they are interpreted in a special sense (i.e., as supernatural "attributes", sometimes capitalized —like Love, Good, Truth— to emphasize the special way in which they apply to God) they cannot be truly predicated of God. To continue the previous example: God *is* not really eternal, but only *appears to be* eternal. While it is true that God has no beginning and end, it is not because God is eternal (i.e., 'infinitely extended in time') but because God is timeless (i.e., 'outside and above time'). In other words, God *is* not eternal, but only *appears to be* eternal because God is supertemporal (i.e., not in time and thus has no beginning or end). In other words, the real attributes try to describe the divine in mundane terms, to describe the supernatural in terms of natural properties, to describe the transcategorical in terms of categorical predicates, i.e., to describe the attributeless in terms of (real) attributes. Of course, this is impossible. So, the real attributes may be real, but they cannot be truly predicated of God.

To summarize this point: God *appears to have* real attributes but does not really *have* them (i.e., they cannot be truly attributed to God). Thus, they too leave God attributeless.

On the one hand, God *appears to have* real attributes, but does not really *have* them..
  (1) God has all supernatural "attributes" (but these are not real attributes).
  (2) God *appears to have* real attributes (but does not really *have* them).
In other words,
  (1) The supernatural "attributes" can be truly attributed of God, but they are not real attributes.
  (1) The real attributes cannot be truly attributed to God.

Notes:
  (a) I use double quotes as a reminder that the supernatural "attributes" are not real attributes. I also use double quotes when I refer to "attributes" in general, to err on the safe side.
  (b) Most of the supposedly real attributes of God can be interpreted both ways, as real attributes and as supernatural "attributes". For example, 'eternal' can be interpreted as a real attribute (i.e., as 'without beginning and end because of being infinitely extended *in* time') or as a supernatural "attribute" (as 'without beginning and end because of being *outside and above* time').
       Of course, if one considers 'eternity' to be an instance of 'infinity', and one agrees that the notion of infinity in general is not a real attribute (e.g., not natural, not categorical, not conceptual; contradictory if treated as a logical, metaphysical, or epistemological concept), it may well be that many of the supposedly real attributes of God are necessarily supernatural "attributes". After all, if real attributes are applied to God, they are often said to apply in *infinite* measure.
  (c) At the end of Part II, we will see even more kinds of "attributes" –

Summary of the general, theoretical explanation

Accepting that God is attributeless, does not reduce God in any way. Quite the opposite! That God is supernatural and thus attributeless means that:

(1) God has all supernatural "attributes".

(2) God *appears to have* all of the real attributes.

So, by claiming that God is attributeless, I do not take away anything from God. In fact, it is only by accepting that God is attributeless (i.e., nothing in particular) that we can see that God is truly infinite (i.e., all in essence) and has all of the typical "attributes" of God.

Specific, practical examples (i.e., the typical "attributes" of God in light of this account of God as supernatural)

In this section, I will show that this is still an account of God by showing that the typical "attributes" of God follow from, or at least cohere with, this account of God as supernatural.

Of course, I cannot discuss all of the typical "attributes" of God because the list is endless. So, I will narrow it down to around 50 of the most common ones. Focusing on the typical "attributes" of the Abrahamic God while including some of the Hindu Godhead (Brahman), and even some "attributes" of the ultimates of non-theistic religions (i.e., the Unconditioned of Buddhism and the Tao of Taoism).

Also, I cannot discuss each "attribute" at length. The "attributes" may well deserve book-length discussions, but those go beyond the scope of this book. So, I will limit myself to one or two paragraphs for each "attribute".

Let me start without further ado.

1.   One

That God is one, can mean at least two things: (i) that God is the one and only God, and (ii) that God is indivisible. Given that God is supernatural, God is one in both senses of the word:

i.   Given that God is supernatural, God is the one and only.

Given that God is supernatural, God is attributeless. Of what is attributeless, there cannot be more than one. Therefore −given that God is supernatural− God is the one and only.

ii.   Given that God is supernatural, God is indivisible.

Given that God is supernatural, God is attributeless. What is attributeless, cannot be analyzed into parts. What cannot be analyzed into parts, is indivisible. Therefore −given that God is supernatural− God is indivisible.

Notes:

    (a) Of what is supernatural, there cannot be more than one. So, if all Gods (and all 'ultimates') are supernatural:

- All religions ultimately concern themselves with the one and only supernatural.
- Polytheism, understood as the belief that there are multiple supernatural beings, is contradictory.
- Forms of monotheism that claim that there are multiple supernatural beings (i.e., not just God, but also e.g., angels) are also contradictory.

2.   Simple

Given that God is supernatural, God is attributeless. What is attributeless, is simple, absolutely simple. Therefore –given that God is supernatural– God is simple.

3.   Absolutely transcendent

Given that God is supernatural, God is outside and above all else. What is outside and above all else, is absolutely transcendent. Therefore –given that God is supernatural– God is absolutely transcendent.

4.   Greater-than-the-greatest

Given that God is supernatural, God is outside and above all else. What is outside and above all else, is not the greatest (among all things) but greater-than-the-greatest (i.e., transcends all thing). Therefore –given that God is supernatural– God is greater-than-the-greatest.

Notes:

    (a) Given that God is supernatural, God is not *primus inter pares* (i.e., first among equals), but absolutely transcendent, outside and above all else, outside and above the greatest of the equals. The tallest man cannot reach heaven, says Proverbs, and so it is: The greatest we can imagine, is not God; God is greater-than-the-greatest.

    (b) St Anselm's ontological argument relies on God being the greatest that can be conceived, but given that God is supernatural, God is greater than the greatest that can be conceived (i.e., inconceivable). Thus, St Anselm's ontological argument cannot prove the existence of God.

5.   King-of-kings, lord-of-lords

These are just metaphorical ways of saying that God is greater-than-the-greatest, i.e., absolutely transcendent, and thus supernatural.

6.   Father, shepherd, lord, king

Given that God is supernatural, above all else, God is like a father, shepherd, lord, king.

Notes:
   (a) Please forgive the outdated view of seeing the father as standing above the family. It just seems to be an aspect of what 'father' means in religious contexts.
   (b) These metaphors only apply if they are understood as ways of saying that God is outside and above the natural, absolutely transcendent. The terms do not apply if they are understood as ways of saying that God is the first among all (natural) things (i.e., a *primus inter pares*).

7.   Supreme, ultimate

Definitions: 'Supreme' is a superlative derived from Latin *super*, meaning 'outside and above'. 'Ultimate' comes from Latin *ulter*, which also means beyond, outside and above.

Rationale: Given that God is supernatural, outside and above all else, God is supreme and ultimate.

8.   Infinite, limitless, unlimited

Given that God is supernatural, God is attributeless. What is attributeless, has no attributes (e.g., no temporal attributes like a beginning, end, or duration; no spatial attributes like a size, shape, or location) and hence no limits. Therefore – given that God is supernatural– God is limit-less, un-limited, in-finite.

Notes:

    (a) Attributes limit. They distinguish a thing from what it is not (e.g., other things, their background) and thereby limits it. As the scholastics put it, *Omnis determinatio est negatio*, all determination is negation.

    (b) 'Infinite' does not mean 'incredibly big', but 'not finite', not limited, limit-less, e.g., dimension-less (in terms of space), beginning-less and end-less and thus duration-less (in terms of time). Thus, 'infinite' can only refer to what lies outside all categories, even outside time and space, i.e., 'infinite' can only refer to what is supernatural. (Not surprisingly, when physicist think about the infinite, they run into similar issues as theologists who think about God: The terms are referentially equivalent.)

9.   Eternal

Given that God is supernatural, God is attributeless, without attributes, and thus also without temporal attributes, for example, without beginning and without end. What has no beginning and no end in time, is infinite and thus appears to be eternal. Therefore –given that God is supernatural– God appears to be eternal.

Notes:

    (a) Of course, in reality, God is not eternal (i.e. infinitely extended in time) but timeless (i.e., outside and above time, not in time, non-temporal), and God only appears to be eternal.

    (b) To say that God is eternal, is just a euphemistic way (if ultimately inadequate) to say that God is super-temporal, and thus super-natural.

10. Universal

Given that God is supernatural, God is attributeless, without attributes, and thus also without spatial attributes, for example, without dimensions (e.g., size, shape, and location). What has no dimensions, is infinite and thus appears to be universal. Therefore –given that God is supernatural– God appears to be universal.

Notes:

    (a) Of course, in reality, God is not universal (i.e. infinitely extended in space) but dimensionless (i.e., outside and above space, not in space, spaceless, non-spatial), and only appears to be universal.

(b) To say that God is universal, is just a euphemistic way (if ultimately inadequate) to say that God is super-spatial, and thus super-natural.

11. Omnipresent (all-present)

Definition: 'Omnipresent' means 'all-present' or, more freely interpreted, 'ever-present', from Latin *omni-*, from *omnis*, meaning 'all, every, always and everywhere', and *praesentem*, meaning 'present' in the sense of '*being* here and now'. So, I take 'omnipresent' to mean 'always-and-everywhere here-and-now'.

Rationale 1: Given that God is supernatural, God is eternal and universal. What is eternal and universal, is omnipresent. Therefore –given that God is supernatural– God is omnipresent.

Rationale 2: Given that God is supernatural, God is identical with *being* (in the thinnest, least weighty sense of the words). *Being* is always-and-everywhere here-and-now, if only because nothing could *be* (or even *appear to be*) without *being*. Therefore –given that God is supernatural– God is omnipresent.

Rationale 3: Given that God is supernatural, God is identical with consciousness (in the thinnest, least weighty sense of the words), and consciousness is always-and-everywhere here-and-now. Consciousness is always-and-everywhere here-and-now, even if it is conscious of thoughts about the past (i.e., memories) or about the future (i.e., anticipations). The past and the future are thoughts that appear in consciousness here and now. The only evidence for what *was* and what *will be*, is what *is* now. What *is* here and now is concrete; what *was* and what *will be* are inferred from what *is* here and now. Therefore –given that God is supernatural– God is omnipresent.

Rationale 4: Given that God is supernatural, God is identical with what I am (in the thinnest, least weighty sense of the words), and what I am is always-and-everywhere here-and-now. I realize this may sound strange at first, but I am only ever here and now. (And I expect you can say the same for yourself.) I am never ever not here or not now. I cannot ever *be* anywhere else than here. I cannot ever *be* anywhen else than now. Wherever I go, by the time I get there, I *am* here and now. Therefore –given that God is supernatural– God is omnipresent.

12. Omniscient (all-knowing)

Definition: 'Omniscient' means 'all-knowing', from Latin *omni-*, meaning 'all, every, always and everywhere', and *scientia*, from *scire*, meaning 'to know'.

Rationale 1: Given that God is supernatural, God is omnipresent. If God is omnipresent, God is omniscient. Therefore –given that God is supernatural– God is omniscient.

Rationale 2:
[1]   Given that God is supernatural, God is consciousness.
[2]   Consciousness is necessarily conscious of the content-of-conscious.
[3]   Consciousness and the content-of-consciousness is all there is. *)
[4]   Thus, consciousness is conscious of all else, i.e., omniscient.
[5]   Therefore –given that God is supernatural– God is omniscient.

Notes:
   *)   One may believe that the content-of-consciousness is caused by an
        underlying, objective reality (i.e., things in themselves, real existents),
        but even if this were the case, we could never know it. Thus, the belief
        that there is anything besides consciousness and content-of-
        consciousness is mere speculation, not only unsupported by reason but
        forever unsupportable by reason, i.e., pure superstition. The assumption
        seems to be based on the illicit inference that, because an appearance
        appears, it must be caused by something else, something of an entirely
        different and forever unknowable order (of things that exists in some
        other way than as appearances). In other words, it is to assume that a
        subjective appearance requires an objective reality. But, for example,
        dreams and hallucinations clearly show that appearances do not require
        an objective reality. In summary, as far as I can tell, consciousness and
        the content-of-conscious are complements in all (i.e., mutually
        exclusive and jointly exhaustive).
   (a) I use 'scient' in the broader, colloquial sense of 'knowing'. That is, in
        the sense of being aware, being conscious. Not in the stricter,
        philosophical sense (e.g., of believing a true proposition to be true for
        the right reasons). However, such a strict sense of 'knowing' is covered
        by the wider sense: If God is conscious of all, God knows all (i.e. is
        conscious of all true propositions and thus also of the fact that they are
        true).

13. Omnipotent (almighty)

Definition: 'Omnipotent' means 'all-potent' or 'all-mighty', from Latin *omni-*, from *omnis*, meaning 'all, every, always and everywhere', and *potentem*, meaning 'potent, powerful, mighty'.

Rationale: There are many ways to interpret this "attribute" and the way it applies to God. Here are some. Given that God is supernatural:
1. God is limitless, not limited in any sense, and thus appears to be omnipotent.
2. God is not subject to the laws of nature, and thus appears to defy the laws of nature, and thus appears to be omnipotent.
3. God is *being*, without which nothing could *be* or even *appear to be*. *Being* is the 'material cause', that which allows all else to *(appear to) be*. Thus, God can be considered to be omnipotent.
4. God is earlier-than-the-earliest, and thus appears to be the earliest, and thus appears to be (the only possible candidate to qualify as) the first cause, and thus appears to be omnipotent.
5. God is uncaused, and thus appears to be (the only possible candidate to qualify as) the uncaused cause, and thus appears to be omnipotent.

It seems the "attribute" is a way of saying that God is the necessary (pre-)condition for all else (e.g., the human being that I took to be myself, other human beings, the world, the universe), of which, projected in time, God is also the sustainer (i.e., that which allows everything else *to be* or, at least, *to appear to be*).

Notes:
(a) Doesn't omnipotence imply participation in causality? No, I consider omnipotence to be a way of saying that *being* (i.e. the supernatural) is the necessary (pre-)condition for all that *appears to be* (i.e., the natural), just like the dreamer is the necessary (pre-)condition for the dream. Such a (pre-)condition is not a link in the causal chain of events, not a causal factor.

14. Omnibenevolent (all-good-willing)

Definition: 'Omnibenevolent' means 'all-well-wishing' or 'all-good-willing', from Latin *omni-*, from *omnis*, meaning 'all, every, always and everywhere', and *benevolent*, meaning 'good-willing', from *bene-*, meaning 'well, good', and *volent*, meaning 'wishing, willing'.

Rationale: Given that God is supernatural, God is *being*, which allows all else *to be*, and thus seems to care for everything, including the human being that I took to be myself, my loved ones, on earth as well as in heaven, and so on. Because God seems to care for all that I care for, I can consider God to be good-willing, well-wishing, i.e., benevolent.

15. Divinely hidden

Given that God is supernatural, God is attributeless. What is attributeless cannot appear (e.g., be perceived) because only attributes can appear. Therefore –given that God is supernatural– God cannot appear, cannot be found, and seems hidden. Moreover –given that God is supernatural– God is not just hidden behind something else but hidden in the uniquely 'divine' way that only God (i.e., the supernatural) is hidden (namely, as the subject). Thus, it can be said that God being divinely hidden.

Notes:
(a) Of course, God is not really hidden. God is the observer that is present in every observation. But the observer cannot observe itself, just because the observer is that which observes (i.e., subject cannot appear to itself – Even if I supposedly think of myself, I observe thoughts (about what I take to be myself), but I do not observe myself; if I look in the mirror, I observe reflections (of what I take to be myself), but I do not observe myself. God is like the eye that can see all except itself.

16. Good

Being is necessary (for myself and all else to be able *to be* or *appear to be*). What is necessary, is what ought to *be*. What ought to *be*, is good. Therefore, *being* is good. Given that God is supernatural, God is identical with *being*. Therefore, God is good.

17. Love

Being allows everything *to (appear to) be*, e.g., the human being that I took myself to be, my loved ones, etc. It seems to "accept" and "care for" everybody and everything, which seems to be an act of love. Moreover, because *being* seems impartial, caring for all things, saints and sinners alike, *being*'s love seems unconditional, i.e., *being* is Love with a capital 'L'. Given that God is supernatural, God is identical with *being*. Subsequently, God is said to be Love.

18. Willful

Being makes it possible for all else to happen and to happen according to certain principles (e.g., the laws of nature), develop in certain directions (e.g., evolution), and demand that things level out, are kept in balance. If one sees intention in this, *being* may seem wilful. Given that God is supernatural, God is identical with *being*. Subsequently, God seems wilful. All seems to happen intentionally, volitionally, 'because God wills it so'.

Notes:
    (a)   In reality, God wills the creation no more than the dreamer wills the dream.

19. Righteous

This follows from the previous point. Given that God is supernatural, God appears to will that things level out, are kept in balance, and thus God appears to be righteous. For example, if you do good, you are more likely to encounter good, whereas, if you do bad, you are more likely to encounter bad. Thus, it seems that bad deeds / people are punished, and good deeds / people are rewarded. There seems to be a law of just retribution. As Sri Nisargadatta put it, 'The healing hand of God demands that the balance be restored'. (Sri Nisargadatta Maharaj, *I am that*, transcribed and translated by Maurice Frydman, edited by Sudhakar S. Dixit, 1973) Since we do not know why this law seems to work in this way, we attribute it to God. If God is the law-giver (e.g., king-of-kings, lord-of-lords), it follows that God must be just (i.e., righteous), either directly or by having built it into the universe, serving each person what (s)he deserves.

The following two points are merely the positive, respectively, negative variants of this same principle.

20. Wrathful, jealous

If supposedly bad deeds appear to be punished, God appears to be wrathful or jealous (either directly or by having it built it into the universe).

21. Merciful, gracious

If supposedly good deeds appear to be rewarded, or supposedly bad deeds appear to be forgiven, God appears to be merciful, gracious (either directly or by having it built it into the universe).

22. Worshipful, worshipable, worthy of devotion

Given that God is supernatural, God is greater-than-the-greatest, righteous, good, merciful, graceful, loving, and so on, a king-of-kings, a lord-of-lords, so God seems worthy of our worship and devotion.

Notes:
   (a) Of course, God does not require or benefit from one's worshipping, but devoting oneself to God is a time-tested path (e.g., Abrahamic religions command us to love God with all our hearts, Hindus call it *bhakti yoga*) that helps us to drop the belief in the separate self, in being a human being, overcoming the apparent separation, and opening the door to union with God. This is not the path that I am "preaching" here. What I am "preaching" here, in this book, is a path of reason (e.g., Abrahamic religions call it the *via negativa*, Hindus call it *jnana yoga*). But the path of devotion may well be more effective.
   (b) Given that God is supernatural, God is identical with what I am, so love and worship of God, is ultimately love and devotion to one's self (i.e., the true self, not the person or the human being I took to be myself). This seems unavoidable. Even altruistic thoughts and actions and suicide (of the person, the human being) may ultimately be motivated by self-love.

23. Immortal, deathless

Rationale 1: Given that God is supernatural, God is not born. What is not born, cannot die. So –given that God is supernatural– God cannot die, God is deathless and will thus appear to be immortal to those who consider God to be alive.

Rationale 2: As we have seen –given that God is supernatural– God is timeless, has no beginning and/or end, and appears to be eternal, and thus immortal, deathless.

Notes:
- (a) God is not something that was born, but (miraculously) cannot die. God is not born, not 'alive' in the sense that human beings and other things appear to be alive. This is the difference between *being* (i.e., what *is*, God) and becoming, living and dying (i.e., what *appears to be*, all else).
- (b) What is not born, cannot die. Likewise: What is not created, cannot be destroyed; What is not caused, cannot disappear into its effect; What is not conditioned, is not conditional, cannot come undone due to changing conditions.

24. Aseity (from *a se*, meaning *being* in/of/by itself)

Given that God is supernatural, God is outside and above all else, not in anything else, not made of anything else, not existing by virtue of anything else. It follows that God is in/of/by itself or, in Latin *a se*, which is called asiety (a-se-ity).

25. Uncaused first cause

Cause: Given that God is supernatural, God is *being(ness)*. *Being(ness)* is a condition for all else and can be considered to be the (material) **cause** of all else. Thus, God can be considered to be the (material) **cause** of all else

Uncaused: Given that God is supernatural, God *is*, but God is not natural, i.e., not born, created, caused, or otherwise conditioned. What *is*, but is not born, created, caused, or otherwise conditioned, must be uncaused. Thus, God is **uncaused**. (This is not to say that God is a thing that is not caused, but that God is not a thing and not caused.)

First: Given that God is supernatural, God appears to be eternal, and thus also appears to be have been earlier-than-the-earliest, i.e., **first**.

So –given that God is supernatural– God appears to be the **uncaused first cause**.

Notes:
- (a) In reality, God is not a cause, but a condition. All causes are conditions, but not all conditions are causes. A condition need not be causal. Where a cause brings about an effect, a condition need not. So, *being* (and thus

God) is a condition for all else (i.e., nothing can *be* or *appear to be* without *being*), but not a cause (i.e., it does not bring about an effect).

(b) In reality, God is not causal, but non-causal, neither cause nor effect. To be causal is to be both cause and effect, and to be non-causal is to be neither cause nor effect. (To suppose differently is to violate the principle of causality, which presumes that every effect must have a cause, and every cause must have an effect, and thus that every cause must have a cause.) Given that God is supernatural, not natural, not caused, God is not causal, i.e., not a causal factor, not a link in the causal chain of events, not causally dependent (on its causes), but non-causal. God is neither a cause nor an effect, and God has neither causes nor effects.

26. Creator

Given that God is supernatural, God is the creator of the heavens and the earth in a similar sense as a dreamer is the creator of the dream.

Notes:

(a) In reality, God does not intentionally create the creation any more than a dreamer intentionally creates the dream. Given that God is supernatural, God is not caused, and thus cannot cause (e.g., create or destroy) but only "allow" things to happen. God is causally impotent. But God is the condition (and perhaps the so-called 'material cause'), ground, essence, subsistence, substance, evidence, for the creation.

27. Perfect

Rationale 1: Given that God is supernatural, God is attributeless, and what is attributeless, is perfect, i.e., complete and flawless.

i. What is attributeless is complete because:
  o To be incomplete (i.e., finite) requires attributes.
  o Nothing can be added to or subtracted from what is attributeless, because only attributes can be added or subtracted.

ii. What is attributeless is flawless because flaws are attributes.

Rationale 2: Given that God is supernatural, God is *being*, and *being* is perfect, i.e., complete and flawless.

28. Unconditioned, unconditional, independent

Given that God is supernatural, not natural, God is not (born, created, caused, or otherwise) conditioned, i.e., God is unconditioned. Given that God is unconditioned, God is not subject to conditions, does not depend on conditions, is not affected by changing conditions, and is thus unconditional, independent.

29. Absolute

Given that God is supernatural, God is unconditioned and unconditional. The word 'absolute' comes from the Latin *absolutus*, from *absolvere*, from *ab-*, meaning 'from, off' and *solvere*, meaning 'to loosen, untie, release, detach, set free from', and thus 'absolute' means 'unconditioned-unconditional'. Therefore –given that God is supernatural– God is unconditioned and unconditional, and thus absolute.

30. Supreme *Being*

Given that God is supernatural, God is identical with *being*. Also –given that God is supernatural– God is *super-*, and thus supreme, because the words *super-* and supreme have the same meaning (although one is word-forming and the other adjectival). *Being* is indeed supreme because it, and it alone, transcends all else. So –given that God is supernatural– God is supreme and *being*, and thus God could be said to be supreme *being*.

Notes:
   (a) Strictly speaking, the word 'supreme' is redundant because *being* is (by definition) supreme.
   (b) To say that God is '(the) Supreme Being' can be (mis)taken to imply (i) that God is a particular being, an individual, an entity, like a human being, and (ii) that God is one being among other beings (albeit the supreme one, the *primus inter pares*). But *being* cannot be divided into multiple beings. *Being* is one and indivisible.
   (c) It may well be that the ambivalence (between God as a being and God as *being*) is exploited to be able to express the ultimate reality without scaring off people who believe that God is a natural (i.e., human-like) being.

31. Subsistence

Definition: 'Subsistence' comes from Latin *sub-*, meaning 'under', and *sistere*, meaning 'to place, to stand', meaning that which stands under, the foundation.

Rationale: Given that God is supernatural, God is identical with *being*. *Being* is that which allows all else *to (appear to) be*, i.e., that which underlies, stands under all else. Therefore –given that God is supernatural– God is subsistence.

Notes:
    (a) In their etymological sense, 'subsistence' is the opposite of 'existence'. Existence comes from Latin *ex-*, meaning 'out of', and *sistere*, 'to place, to stand', and thus means that which 'stands forth, emerges, appears out of'. Where 'subsistence' refers to what underlies all else (i.e., what *is, being*), 'existence', refers to what emerges from it (i.e., what *appears to be*, all else). In this sense, *being* sub-sists all that ex-sists. I.e., all that ex-sists (i.e., all that *appears to be*, the creation) emerges from what sub-sists it (i.e., *being*, God). It is like the difference as between '*being*' and 'becoming'.

    (b) While 'super-natural' sounds more respectful, we could just as well say that God is 'sub-natural', as the point is that God is 'not-natural'.

32. Essence

Definition: 'Essence' means '*being*'. 'Essence' comes from Latin *essentia*, meaning '*being*', from *esse*, meaning '*to be*'. The word was used to translate the Greek notion of *ousia*, meaning '*being*', into Latin.

Rationale: Given that God is supernatural, God is identical with *being,* i.e., with (the) essence. And, indeed, God is the essence (i.e., *being(ness)*) of itself and of all that *appears to be*.

33. Substance

Definition: 'Substance' comes from Latin *sub-*, meaning 'under', and *stare*, meaning 'to stand'. Etymologically, it is synonymous with subsistence. Colloquially, it refers to the material out of which a thing is made. So, the substance of a clay pot is clay.

Rationale: Given that God is supernatural, God is identical with consciousness and all else is content-of-consciousness. (See chapter 7.) The content-of-consciousness consists of nothing but consciousness. In other words, consciousness is the substance of the content-of-consciousness. Given that consciousness and the content-of-consciousness is all there is, consciousness is the substance of all else. Therefore –given that God is supernatural– God is the substance of all else.

Notes:
   (a) I do not use the term 'substance' in the Aristotelian sense. Aristotle used the term 'substance' to denote the supposed essence (as opposed to the properties) of individual things (i.e., objects, beings, individuals, particulars) rather than for the base material(s) out of which individual things are made. Subsequently, he assumed that there are many, individual substances. I disagree with this view and do not use the term 'substance' in the Aristotelian sense. On my view, there are no individual substances. There *are* no individual objects; individual objects only *appear to be*. The substance (in the Aristotelian sense, i.e., essence, *being*) that individual objects may appear to have, does not belong to the individual objects, but to the subject (i.e., *being*). *Being* is one and indivisible. The essence (i.e., *being*) of all objects is the subject (i.e., *being*).

34. Evidence

Definition: 'Evidence' comes from Latin *ex-*, meaning 'out of', and *videre*, meaning 'to see', so 'evidence' means 'what can be inferred out of seeing'.

Rationale: Given that God is supernatural, God is consciousness. Consciousness is that which is the witness, the evidence(r), of all that it is conscious of (and to suppose there is more than consciousness and what consciousness is conscious of, is an assumption that cannot *ever* be verified, mere superstition, and does not belong in rational discourse). Therefore, God is the witness, the evidence(r) of all else.

35. Incorporeal

Definition: 'Incorporeal' means 'without body', from Latin *incorporeus*, from *in-*, meaning 'not' and *corpus*, meaning 'body'.

Rationale: Given that God is supernatural, God is not natural, not physical, not a body.

Notes:
    (a) Of course –given that God is supernatural– God is not just in-corpo-real (i.e., not-em-bodied) but also im-menta-real (i.e., not-em-minded), so to speak. God is neither physical nor mental, neither body nor mind.

36. Person

Definition: 'Person' means 'personage, human being', from Latin *persona*, originally meaning 'mask, fake face', like the masks worn by the actors in a play, later coming to mean 'assumed character, a part in a play', and finally, 'personage, human being, person'.

Rationale 1: Given that God is supernatural, God can appear as a person (i.e., embodied, incarnated, corporeal), that is, God can appear to act through a body (for example, the body of Christ, Krishna, etc.).

Rationale 2: Given that God is supernatural, God is what I am, and thus God may seem to experience the world through the body of Ruud.

Notes:
    (a) Given that God is supernatural, not natural, God is not a person, not a personage, not a human being, neither body nor mind, neither a living organism nor any role or function(ing) thereof, nor otherwise endowed with (anthropomorphic) qualities. To portray God as a person, is to jeopardize the very purpose of religion.
    (b) I may have mistakenly identified myself with the human being, but it is not what I am. God may speak through a human being, but God is not that human being.

37. Spirit, spiritual

Given that God is supernatural, God is neither physical nor mental, but spiritual, so to speak, or neutral (as in neutral monism).

38. Holy Spirit

Given that God is supernatural, God is neither body nor mind, but spirit. And since God is also considered to be holy, we can say that God is (the) Holy Spirit.

Notes:
    (a) The term is somewhat unfortunate because it seems to objectivize the spirit(ual) and thus God, while the spirit(ual) is not an object, neither a physical nor a mental object. The very point of the word 'spiritual' is to distinguish God from the physical and the mental.

39. Holy Ghost

I suppose that, since in other contexts, the terms 'ghosts' and 'spirits' are used interchangeably, the terms 'Holy Spirit' and 'Holy Ghost' came to be used inter-changeably.

Notes:
    (a) The term 'ghost' is perhaps even more unfortunate than 'spirit'. Not only does it seem to objectivize the spiritual, it also evokes images of, e.g., an amorph thing that flies around in a white sheet, while God cannot be imagined, but is inconceivable, unimaginable.

40. Soul

Given that God is supernatural, God is neither body nor mind, but soul, so to speak.

Notes:
    (a) Some people believe that there are multiple souls (i.e., that each human being has an individual soul). But is there any reason to believe that there are multiple souls? If we cannot even be certain that there are other minds (cf., 'the problem of other minds' and 'the distribution problem of consciousness' in the philosophy of mind), how can we be certain that there are other souls? If we cannot be certain, the belief in multiple/other souls is unsupported by reason, a form of superstition.
    (b) Some people believe that the soul is created (e.g., that a fetus gets a soul at some point in its development), but if we cannot be certain that there are multiple/other souls, then neither can we be certain that any souls

are created. Moreover, people who believe that the soul is created also tend to believe that the soul does not perish (not even if its supposed host dies) but that the soul goes on into an (eternal) after-life. This seems contradictory to me, because, to my knowledge, all that is created, also perishes. Everything is either causal or non-causal. Also, it is 'a monstrous thought', as Arthur Schopenhauer put it. Others believe that the soul is a 'spark of God'. If this means that it is to be re-united with God upon death of its host, that would be one step forward compared to the previous view. But the soul is not just a spark of God, the soul is identical with God, and the (re-)union does not have to wait until the body dies but can be realized right here and now.

41. Trinity (i.e., Father, Son, and Holy Spirit)

Given that God is supernatural:
  (1) God is like a Father (see attribute 6),
  (2) God can seem to act through a human being, acting on God's behalf, sent by God, e.g., a Son, (see attribute 36), and
  (3) God can be said to be (the) Holy Spirit (see attribute 38).

42. Lux perpetua

Definition: *Lux* is Latin, meaning 'light'. *Perpetua* is also Latin, meaning 'perpetual, everlasting, continuous, universal'. Thus, *lux perpetua* means 'everlasting light'.

Rationale: Given that God is supernatural, God is *being*, which is the *being* of all that appears to be, and which can be expressed metaphorically as the light (i.e., *lux*) in which all else appears. While all else appears and disappears in the light, the light itself remains, lasts (i.e., is *perpetua*).

43. Requiem aeternam

Definition: *Requiem* is Latin, meaning 'rest'. *Aeternam* is Latin, meaning 'eternal'. So, *requiem aeternam* means eternal rest.

Rationale: Given that God is supernatural, God is *being*. While all that *appears to be*, comes and goes, appears and disappears (e.g., is born and dies), *being* itself is eternally (i.e., *aeternam*) at rest (i.e., *requiem*). Thus, God is eternally at rest. Given that what I am is God, it also grants me eternal rest.

44. Immutable

Definition: 'Immutable' means 'incapable of change'. From Latin *in-* 'not' and *mutabilis* 'capable of change', from *mutare* 'to change'.

Rationale: Given that God is supernatural, God is attributeless. What is attributeless, cannot change because all change is of attributes. So –given that God is supernatural– God is incapable of change, i.e., immutable.

45. Impassible

Definition: 'Impassible' means 'incapable of suffering'. From Latin *in-* 'not' and *passibilis* 'capable of suffering', from *passio* 'suffering'.

Rationale: Given that God is supernatural, God is neither physical nor mental, neither body nor mind, and is thus incapable of suffering, i.e., impassible.

46. Indescribable, incomparable, incomprehensible

Given that God is supernatural, God is attributeless. What is attributeless, is indescribable (because descriptions require attributes), incomparable (because all comparison is of attributes), and incomprehensible (because all comprehension is of attributes).

Notes:
   (a) This is not to say that God cannot be 'described' of 'defined' in other ways. For example, negatively, by saying what God is not (i.e., *via negativa, neti neti*) and extensionally (i.e., referentially, e.g., by means of synonyms). But these are not considered to be proper 'descriptions' or 'definitions' because they do not define a term by listing its genera-differentiae, they are not intensional, not qualitative.

47. Hinduism: *sat-chit-ananda*

According to Hinduism, we cannot really describe God (because all descriptions are of some things in terms of other things, while God is not a thing). The closest we can come, is to say that God is *satchitananda*. The term *satchitananda* is a portmanteau of three terms: *sat*, *chit*, and *ananda*. *Sat* means something like *being*, what *is*, what is real. *Chit* means something like consciousness, awareness, what knows, what is known, what is true. *Ananda* means something like peace, what is good. Thus, *satchitananda* means something like being-consciousness-peace or real-true-good.

Sat

Given that God is supernatural, God is identical with *being*, with what is real, i.e., **sat**.

Chit

Given that God is supernatural, God is identical with consciousness, i.e., ***chit***.

Ananda

Rationale 1: Given that God is supernatural, God is identical with *being*, i.e., with what is real. What is real cannot change (and what changes is not real). *Being* cannot change because being is attributeless and all change is of attributes. Therefore, God cannot change, but is at peace, i.e., ***ananda***.

Rationale 2: Given that God is supernatural, God is identical with *being*, with what *is*. What *is*, is what ought to *be*, i.e., what is good. Therefore, God is good, i.e., ***ananda***.

48. Taoism: The way that cannot be walked, told, or named

Given that God is supernatural, outside and above the natural, there is no way one can walk to reach God, as God cannot be located or found among natural things. (In the dream of waking life there is no path that can lead one to the dreamer because the dreamer cannot be found in the dream. One need not go anywhere in the dream of waking life, but merely wake up to the dream of waking life. That is, to realize that waking life is a dream-like experience of which one is conscious, but of which one is not a part. To realize this is peace.)

Given that God is supernatural, and thus transconceptual, what God is, cannot be told, at least not in the usual way, conceptually.

Given that God is supernatural, God cannot be located, singled out, picked out, pointed out, determined, identified as one thing among other things, which is what I take 'named' to mean in verse 1 of the Tao Te Ching. (Strictly speaking, I believe God can be named (I just did) and identified (e.g., as supernatural and as *being*) because identity does not require predicates ("sense") but can (non-conceptually) be established by use of synonyms and referential equivalents.)

49. Buddhism: unborn, deathless, unconditioned; empty

Given that God is supernatural, God is not natural, not born, i.e., **unborn**.

Given that God is supernatural, God is not born. What is not born, cannot die. Therefore –given that God is supernatural– God cannot die, i.e., is **deathless**.

Given that God is supernatural, God is not natural, not conditioned, i.e., **unconditioned**.

Given that God is supernatural, God is attributeless, i.e., **empty, emptiness**.

Conclusion of Part II.

I hope to have illustrated that the typical "attributes" of God can be seen as ways or attempts, if sometimes inadequate, to say that God is supernatural, i.e., that the "attributes" follow from (or at least cohere with) the notion of God as supernatural. There are different kinds:

(1) Supernatural "attributes", which God really *has.*

These consist of all synonyms and referential equivalents of 'supernatural', for example, 'transcategorical', 'attributeless', 'transconceptual', and 'extraordinary'; 'being(ness)', 'consciousness', and 'what I am'; and 'infinite', 'greater-than-the-greatest' and 'supreme'.

These "attributes" can truly be said of God, but they are not real attributes. They are neither (real, natural) properties nor (real, categorical) predicates. Hence the double-quotes when I refer to "attributes" in general. They are merely different ways of saying that God is supernatural, i.e., attributeless.

(2) Real attributes, which God merely *appears to have.*

These are the real attributes (i.e., (natural) properties and/or (categorical) predicates) that are typically attributed of God, for example, 'creator', 'first cause', 'eternal', and 'good'.

God does not really *have* these attributes, but only *appears to have* them. For example: God does not really have the attribute of being 'eternal' (i.e., of being infinitely extended in time). But, given that God is supernatural, attributeless, without attributes, and thus also without temporal attributes, without beginning and end, God *appears to have* the attribute of being 'eternal' (because what is without beginning and end will *appear to be* eternal). In other words, given that God is supernatural (i.e., outside and above the natural), God is also supertemporal (i.e., outside and above time); Given that God is supertemporal, God has no beginning or end in time; Given that God has no beginning or end in time, God *appears to be* eternal.

In this way, all of the typical real attributes of God, follow from the fact that God is supernatural and thus attributeless.

The real attributes describe how God appears to me when I look at God through the eyes of man, i.e., when I try to describe the attributeless in terms of attributes, the transcategorical in terms of genera and differentiae, the transconceptual in terms of predicates, the supernatural in terms of natural properties. They are just ways or attempts (if ultimately inadequate) of saying that God is supernatural. They may point in the right direction but, strictly speaking, they remain relative.

(3) Superlatives and super-superlatives.

Merely superlative attributes, like 'the greatest' or 'the most perfect', are real attributes that cannot truly be attributed of God. They denote a *primus inter pares* (greatest among equals), while God is *super-pares* (outside and above all equals). Only super-superlatives, like 'greater-than-the greatest', can truly be attributed of God.

(4) Metaphors.

Metaphors can be real attributes or supernatural "attributes". Metaphors like 'king-of-kings' and 'lord-of-lords' are supernatural "attributes", similar to 'greater-than-the-greatest'. These are "attributes" that God really has, but they are not real attributes. But metaphors like 'king', 'lord', and 'father' are natural attributes, similar to 'the greatest'. These are real attributes, but God does not really *have* them; God only *appears to have* them. Metaphors like 'shepherd' can be interpreted both ways.

(5) Negating attributes.

Negating or negative attributes are special and of great importance. They are of great importance because they are the basis of some the oldest and most effective paths to God. For example, the *via negativa* ('negative way'), as it is known in Abrahamic traditions, and the *neti neti* ('not this, not this') and *viveka-vairagya* ('investigate and discard'), as it is known in Hinduism.

Rather than saying what God is, negating attributes are saying what God is not. For example, to say that God is 'incomparable', is to say that God is not comparable, beyond comparison. Negating attributes are typically formed of negating word-forming elements like 'in-', 'im-', '-less', 'ab-', 'a-', 'un-', and so on. For example, 'infinite', 'indivisible', 'incomprehensible', 'immortal', 'deathless', 'absolute', 'atemporal', and 'unconditioned'.

Negating attributes are special because they can be truly attributed of God, even though they are *real* attributes. Because they are real attributes, they are not as weird as supernatural "attributes". Because they can be truly attributed of God, we need not have any reservations regarding their validity. Thus, focusing on negating attributes can be an honest, user-friendly path to God. Moreover, negative paths can start off with fairly obvious claims (e.g., that God is not a giraffe; that God is not a horse; that God is not a dog, etc.). After a while, such particular denials beg one to infer more sweeping, categorical denials (e.g., that God is not an animal). This gentle practice can be applied to every category, e.g., of things, events, processes, thoughts, feelings, etc. If one thus exhausts all categories, one can hardly avoid inferring the most universal denial: that God is not a thing, neither anything in particular, nor merely everything. Such a universal denial may seem to leave us without anything and cause despair. It is sometimes called a 'dark night of the soul'. This expression not only describes the feeling of despair but also hints at the way out: When everything is negated, what remains is the soul. After all, it is a dark night *of the soul*. Without me, without a soul, there could not be a dark night.

So, by negating everything, the barriers to seeing what God is, are gently dismantled. And that is all that is required. God is hidden in plain sight. If one does not see God, it is because one is deceived by appearances, because one suffers from a case of mistaken identity. Because one takes the appearances to be real and identifies oneself with those appearances, instead of identifying oneself with that in and to which the appearances appear, which is before they appeared and after they disappeared (to explain it provisionally, in temporal terms). To see and be God, we only need to remove a misunderstanding that blocks our view. That misunderstanding is what expelled us from paradise. Once it is removed, it gives way to the flip-side of the negative conclusion: The realization that, when the light does not fall on anything and darkness is complete, the light is still shining, it is just not reflected. That light is "prior" to all things, "earlier" than all thoughts, more "intimate" than all feelings, more "essential" than body and mind. It is before anything appeared and after everything disappears. It is my essence (i.e. being(ness)), my awareness (i.e. consciousness), what I am (i.e., soul, spirit, neutral). For an analogy that explains this, see the notes to this section.

While this may work wonderfully, in the ultimate analysis, all negating attributes may well turn out to be supernatural "attributes", not real attributes. Because they do *not* accuse a subject-term of belonging in certain categories, but accuse a subject-term of *not* belonging in certain categories. At least collectively, they negate that God belongs in *any* category whatsoever, i.e., that God is outside and above *all* categories, i.e., that God is transcategorical, supernatural. In a similar way, it may turn out that all real attributes of God are negating (if only because real attributes limit and thus can ultimately only be applied to God in sofar as they are negative).

There is a lot of work that can be done in this area. Although it is not critical, it is certainly interesting.

Notes:
  (a) "Like a light on my head":
      It is as if I am unaware of wearing a light on my head that illuminates all things. Thus, wherever I look, I illuminate all things and I never see anything that is not illuminated. Subsequently, I may come to believe that the things I see, give light (i.e. have light in themselves, and also shine when I do not see them). But, of course, it is my light in which they appear, that gives them whatever light they appear to have. I am the light of all things that appear to me. The light that a thing appears to give is real, but it is not the light of the thing, it is my light.
      Likewise, it is as if I am unaware that I give *being* to all things. Thus, whatever appears to me, appears to have *being* and I never see anything that does not appear to have *being*. Subsequently, I have come to believe that the things that *appear to me, are* (i.e. have *being* in themselves, and also *are* when they do not *appear to me*). But, of course, it is my *being* in which they *appear to be*, my *being* that gives them whatever *being* they appear to have. I am the *being* of all things that *appear to me* (i.e., it is my *being* in which they *appear to be*). The *being* that a thing appears to have is real, but it is not the *being* of the thing, it is my *being*.

In Part II of this account of God as supernatural, I hope to have shown that the typical "attributes" of God can be seen as (e.g., direct, natural, metaphorical, euphemistic, partial, negative) ways or attempts to say that God is supernatural. In fact, most of the typical "attributes" seem to follow from the fact that God is supernatural. Thus, the often apparently conflicting "attributes" of God turn out to be expressions of one and the same proposition (i.e., idea).

SUMMARY

God	All else
Part I That God is supernatural and what it means for God to be supernatural	
1. Supernatural	**1. Natural**
God is outside and above the natural, i.e., outside and above all that is born, created, caused, or otherwise conditioned, i.e., outside and above all else, e.g., outside and above all that is physical and/or mental, outside and above all that is subject to space, time, and/or causality, i.e., outside and above all things.	All else is natural, i.e., born, created, caused, or otherwise conditioned, physical and/or mental, subject to space, time, and/or causality, a thing.
God is not natural, i.e., not born, created, caused, or otherwise conditioned, i.e., not like anything else, e.g., neither physical nor mental (but neutral, spiritual), neither temporal, nor spatial, nor causal (but unconditional), i.e., not a thing.	Idem the above.

Anything that is natural, i.e., anything that is born, created, caused, or otherwise conditioned, i.e., anything else, e.g., anything that is physical and/or mental, anything that is subject to time, space, or causality, i.e., any thing, is not God.	Idem the above.
God is not born and thus cannot die, not created and thus cannot be destroyed, not caused and thus cannot disappear into its effect, and not otherwise conditioned and thus cannot change. God is not subject to the laws of nature. God is unconditioned, unconditional, absolute. God does not have (real, natural) properties. God does not have a nature (i.e., essential properties).	All else is born and will die, created and will perish, caused and will disappear into its effect, or otherwise conditioned and will change when its conditions change. All else is subject to the laws of nature All else is conditioned, conditional, relative. All else has (real, natural) properties. All else has a nature (i.e., essential properties).

Examples in terms of time	
God is outside and above time.	All else is in time.
God is not extended in time.	All else is extended in time.
God has no beginning or end, no duration.	All else has a beginning and end, duration.
God is not temporal, but non-temporal, timeless.	All else is temporal, time-bound.
God is omnipresent (temporally). God is now, only ever now.	All else is not omnipresent (temporally) All else is in the past or future.

God seems eternal (infinitely extended in time).	All else is transient (finite in time)

Examples in terms of space	

God is outside and above space.	All else is in space (assuming that 'space' includes mental space).
God is not extended in space.	All else is extended in space.
God has no size or shape, dimensions, location.	All else has a beginning, end, dimensions, location.
God is not spatial, non-spatial, spaceless.	All else is spatial, space-bound.
God is omnipresent (spatially).	All else is not omnipresent (spatially).
God seems universal (infinitely extended in space).	All else is particular (finite in space)

Examples in terms of causality	

God is outside and above causality.	All else is in causality.
God is not extended in causality, not a link in the causal chain of events, not a causal factor.	All else is extended in causality, a link in the causal chain of events, a causal factor.
God is neither cause nor effect.	All else is both cause and effect.
God has neither causes nor effects.	All else has both causes and effects.

God is not causal, non-causal, uncaused.	All else is causal, caused.
God is not determined, not limited (but limitless, unlimited, infinite), neither in space, time, nor causality.	All else is determined, limited (i.e., finite), in space, time, and/or causality.
2. Transcategorical	**2. Categorical**
God is outside and above the categorical, outside and above the categories, outside and above all genera-differentiae, outside and above all predicates. God is not categorical, no genera-differentiae can be predicated of God. No (real, categorical) predicates can be predicated of God (i.e., God is predicateless). Anything that is categorical, is not God. Anything that belongs in the categories, is not God. Anything of which genera-differentiae can be predicated, is not God, nothing can be predicated of God, God is predicateless.	All else is categorical, belongs in the categories, has genera-differentiae, has predicates.
Predicate and other categorical logics cannot deal with God.	Predicate and other categorical logics can deal with all else.
God cannot be defined categorically (i.e., in terms of genera-differentiae), thus God has no intensional meaning (i.e., no Sinn, 'sense', qualitative identity).	All else can be defined categorically (i.e., in terms of genera-differentiae), thus all else has intensional meaning (i.e., no Sinn, 'sense', qualitative identity).

3. Transconceptual	3. Conceptual
God is not conceptual, conceivable	All else is conceptual, conceivable.
God cannot be conceptualized, conceived.	All else can be conceptualized, conceived.
God is not a concept.	
God cannot be defined (conceptually, as a subject-term of which genera-differentiae are predicated).	All else can be defined (conceptually, as a subject-term of which genera-differentiae are predicated).
God cannot be known (conceptually).	All else can be known (conceptually).
God has no conceptual meaning.	All else has conceptual meaning.
St Anselm's ontological argument does not work	
4. Attributeless	**4. Not attributeless**
God has no (real, natural) properties (i.e., distinguishing features) and no (real, categorical) predicates (i.e., genera-differentiae), so God is attributeless.	All else has (real, natural) properties (i.e., distinguishing features) and (real, categorical) predicates (i.e., genera-differentiae), so all else is not attributeless.
God is simple.	All else is complex.
God is the one and only God.	
5. Extraordinary	**5. Ordinary**

God is out of the ordinary, outside and above the natural order, outside and above the categorical order, outside and above the conceptual order.	All else is ordinary, of the natural order, of the categorical order, of the conceptual order.
6. God is *being(ness)*.	6. All else *appears to be*.
7. God is consciousness.	7. All else is content-of-consciousness.
8. God is what I am.	8. All else is not what I am.
9. God *is* (i.e., exists, is real).	9. All else *is* not.
10. God is essential.	10. All else is not essential.
11. God is good.	

Part II
The typical "attributes" of God
in light of this account of God as supernatural

One.	Many, multiplicity.
Simple (i.e., without attributes).	Complex (i.e., with attributes).
Absolutely transcendent.	Relative to other things.
Greater-than-the-greatest.	Things among other things, if perhaps great or the greatest, *primus inter pares.*
King-of-kings, lord-of-lords.	Kings, lords, and other subjects.
King, lord, shepherd, father (if seen as absolutely transcendent).	Subjects, children.
Supreme, ultimate.	A thing among other things.
Infinite, limitless, unlimited.	Finite, limited, determined.
Eternal.	Limited in time.
Universal.	Limited in space.
Omnipresent.	Then and there.
Omniscient.	Having (supposed) knowledge of good and evil.
Omnipotent.	(Necessarily) impotent.
Omnibenevolent.	No unconditional good-will.
Divinely hidden.	Apparent.

Good.	
Love.	
Willful.	Subject to the will (over which it has no control).
Righteous.	Subject to the (divinely issued) laws of nature.
Wrathful, jealous.	Subject to the (divinely issued) laws of nature.
Merciful, gracious.	Petty.
Worshipful, worshipable, worthy of devotion.	
Immortal, deathless.	Mortal, subject to death.
Aseity (i.e., in/of/by itself).	Due to something else.
Uncaused first cause.	Causal factor, link in the causal chain of events.
Creator.	Created.
Perfect, imperfectible.	Imperfect, perfectible.
Unconditioned, unconditional, independent.	Conditioned, conditional, dependent.
Absolute.	Relative.
Supreme Being.	Relative thing.
Subsistence, essence, substance, evidence.	Existence, appearance, form, evidenced.
Incorporeal (and in-mental-real).	Corporeal and/or mentareal.

Impersonal.	Personal.
Spiritual (i.e., holy spirit, holy ghost).	Physical and/or mental.
Holy Spirit, Holy Ghost.	Body-mind / mind-matter.
Soul.	Body and/or mind.
Trinity.	
Lux perpetua.	Illuminated by the lux perpetua.
Requiem aeternam.	Disquietude (i.e., swayed by the passions).
Immutable (e.g., unchangeable, unmovable).	Changing, moving.
Impassible.	Subject to the passions, desiring and fearing, suffering.
Indescribable, incomparable, incomprehensible.	Describable, comparable, comprehensible.
Being, consciousness, peace.	Appearance, content-of-consciousness, stress.
The way that cannot be walked, told, or named.	What can be walked, told, nor named.

IS IT SUCCESSFUL?

For an account of God to be successful, it must yield a positive answer to the following questions:

1. Is the basic proposition readily and widely acceptable?
    > E.g., is it intuitive, is it not *prima facie* contradictory?

2. Is the account coherent?
    > E.g., is it a uniform whole, is it internally and externally consistent?

3. Is the account complete?
    > E.g., is it not omitting any essential or problematic issues?

1. Is the basic proposition readily and widely acceptable?

For the account to be successful, the basic notion of God that underlies the account should be readily and widely acceptable to the intended audience. Ideally, it should be intuitive and not *prima facie* contradictory. For example, while the claim that 'God is simple' is logically equivalent with the claim that 'God is supernatural', the claim that 'God is simple' is far less intuitive. Also, the claim that 'God is simple' seems *prima facie* contradictory (i.e., how can God be simple yet have so many attributes?) while the claim that 'God is supernatural' does not (i.e., God is supernatural and thus has supernatural attributes). Thus, all else being equal, the claim that 'God is supernatural' is preferable over the claim that 'God is simple'.

The most accurate expression of the proposition (i.e., idea) that underlies this account may well be that:

[1]   What is not supernatural, is not what is God.

But I generally express it as follows:

[1']   God is supernatural.

This proposition is readily and widely acceptable (i.e., intuitive, not *prima facie* contradictory) to the intended audience (i.e., everybody, everywhere, at all times, regardless of religion or denomination, and regardless of whether they believe that God exists). Practically everybody considers God to be supernatural. All Gods are supernatural, in at least some ways. The proposition may even be analytic (e.g., true by definition, necessarily, knowable *a priori* and with certainty).

2. Is the account coherent?

For the account to be successful, it should be coherent. With 'coherent', I mean forming a unified whole and being internally and externally consistent. With 'unified whole', I mean that the statements that make up the account deal with one and the same subject matter or are otherwise related (i.e., have subject- and/or predicate-terms in common). With 'internally consistent', I mean that the statements that make up the account do not contradict each other. With 'externally consistent', I mean that the statements that make up the account do not contradict other statements that are (known to be) true. So, an account of God is consistent if all statements are consistent with the basic idea, with each other, and with all other statements that are (known to be) true.

The account of God as supernatural is indeed a unified whole. First, because all statements that make up the account deal with the same subject matter: God. Second, because the statements that make up the logical-philosophical part of the account of God as supernatural, follow directly from the basic idea (i.e., proposition [1]), and even the typical "attributes" can be seen as ways or attempts to say that God is supernatural. Third, because practically all statements that make up the account are in fact logical equivalents, i.e., all statements express one and the same idea. All statements explain each other.

Since practically all statements that make up the account are logical equivalents, of course, the account is also internally consistent. The statements are merely different ways of expressing the same idea.

The last requirement, of external consistency, is also met because all of the logical equivalent statements that make up the account, express one and the same idea that is (known to be) true. For example, because it is logically equivalent with the statement that 'I am' which is literally self-evident and cannot be denied without contradiction. Thus, the account (as a whole) also corresponds to reality, to what is real, to what *is*.

In summary: The account of God as supernatural is coherent because practically all statements that make up the account are logically equivalent with the basic proposition that is (known to be) true.

Notes:

    (a) Arguably, the one idea underlying this account of God, is the one and only idea that can be known to be true, absolutely true.

3. Is the account complete?

To be successful, the account should cover all angles, also possibly inconvenient ones. Of course, no account is ever absolutely complete. But this account goes a long way towards achieving completeness. (If important angles are missing, please let me know: ruud.schuurman@linea-recta.com)

The basic statement that God is supernatural allows for a complete account of God because it is logically equivalent with the most profound idea of God, that is, that God is attributeless. One cannot go deeper (i.e., more profound) than that.

Besides these three basic requirements, the account of God also yields a positive answer to these questions:

4. Does the account also deal with the issue of God's existence?

5. Is the basic notion of God clear, unambiguous, informative?

While these may not be necessary conditions for an account of God, they contribute to the success of the account.

4. Does the account also deal with God's existence?

An account of God that also deals with God's existence is preferable over one that does not. If God's essence (i.e., God's *being*) and God's existence (i.e., God's *being*, reality) are necessarily interwoven, an account that cannot demonstrate God's *being* seems to fail in an important respect.

The account of God as supernatural does indeed deal with the existence of God. (See chapter 9.) In summary: God is supernatural; of what is supernatural, there cannot be more than one; the one and only supernatural demonstrably exists; therefore, God exists.

5. Is the basic notion of God clear, unambiguous, and informative?

An account of God that is based on a clear, unambiguous, and informative notion of God is preferable over one that is not. The basic notion in this account of God as supernatural is 'supernatural'.

5.1 'Supernatural' is clear

'Supernatural' means 'outside and above the natural', i.e., 'outside and above all that is born, created, caused, or otherwise conditioned'. (See chapter 1.)

5.2 'Supernatural' is unambiguous

'Supernatural' has a single meaning. There is no need to spell 'supernatural' with a capital 's' or otherwise qualify it (e.g., by adding 'divine') to distinguish its meaning in this context from its meaning in other contexts.

Notes:
    (a) In popular culture (e.g., a Netflix series), 'supernatural' is sometimes used as a synonym of 'paranormal'. It is said of natural phenomena that are not (readily) explainable (yet). This is an erroneous use of the term.
    (b) The implications of being supernatural are not always thought through. Thus, people may fail to notice that supernatural and natural are mutually exclusive, and that there cannot be more than one of what is supernatural. This does not mean that the notion can be understood in multiple ways, but rather that the notion is not always properly understood. Also, people who used to believe that God was supernatural

as well as natural, and then realize that the two are mutually exclusive, almost unanimously prefer to uphold that God is supernatural and deny that God is natural. Similarly, people who used to believe that there were multiple supernatural beings (i.e., not just God, but also, e.g., angels), and then realize that there cannot be more than one of what is supernatural, almost unanimously prefer to maintain that God is supernatural, and, at least to date, nobody denied that God is supernatural.

5.3 'Supernatural' is informative

'Supernatural' immediately explains:
1. What is opposed to what (i.e., natural vs. supernatural).
2. What it is that God transcends (i.e., the natural).
3. That God's transcendence is absolute (i.e., that God is outside the natural).
4. Which "attributes" God has (i.e., all and only supernatural "attributes").

Summary of the chapter

I consider this account of God as supernatural to be successful because:
1. The basic proposition is readily and widely acceptable.
2. The account is coherent.
3. The account complete.
And in addition:
4. The account also deals with the issue of God's existence.
5. The basic notion of 'supernatural' is clear, unambiguous, and informative.

CONCLUSION

In this account of God, I argued that God is supernatural and explained what it means for God to be supernatural. I argued by natural means (i.e., by means that are in accordance with contemporary methods and standards of rationality as they are used in the natural sciences, as opposed to supernatural means, e.g., divine revelation), which is what I mean with the account being natural.

In the first part of the account, I argued that God is supernatural, and showed that −given that God is supernatural− God is transcategorical, transconceptual, attributeless, and extraordinary. Each of these indicates the fundamental difference between God and all else: All else is natural, God is not; all else is categorical, God is not; all else is conceptual, God is not; all else has attributes, God does not; all else belongs to the normal order of things, God does not. In the first part, I also showed that God is referentially equivalent with some familiar notions, like *being*, consciousness, and what I am. From these notions, it follows that God *is* (i.e., exists, is real), is essential, and is good. In the course of the first part of the account, I also clarified some historically important issues, e.g., that −given that God is supernatural− there cannot be more than one God, and that that one God exists.

In the second part, I discussed the typical "attributes" of God in light of the account of God as supernatural. I showed that the typical "attributes" of the Abrahamic God (of Judaism, Christianity, and Islam), of the Hindu Godhead (i.e., Brahman), and even of the ultimates of Taoism (i.e., the Tao) and Buddhism (i.e., the Unborn, Deathless, Unconditioned) can be seen as ways or attempts, if ultimately inadequate, to say that God is supernatural.

In the subsequent section, I argued that the account is successful because: The basic idea that underlies the account (i.e., that God is supernatural) is readily and widely acceptable (i.e., intuitive and not *prima facie* contradictory). The account is coherent (i.e., a unified whole, internally and externally consistent). And the account is complete (i.e., covering all angles). In addition to these basic criteria for success, the basic notion is clear, unambiguous, and informative. And the account removes all doubt regarding the existence of God. So, not only does the account appear to be successful as such, it also has some important advantages over the doctrine of divine simplicity and other candidates.

All in all, I believe that one is face with just two options: (1) reject the underlying assumption that God is supernatural, or (2) accept the account of God as supernatural in its entirety.

I hope that this book will challenge you to consider the matter for yourself, and may help you to attain salvation, divine union, enlightenment, liberation, wisdom, or whatever you call *that* which sets you free. Free from sin and the consequences of sin, free from separation, free from craving and ignorance and the pain it causes, free from the cycle of birth and death and its suffering, or, to put it in somewhat plainer terms, free from the stress that comes from being deceived by appearances.

APPENDICES

Appendix 1: Surely, God is more than just attributeless!

That God is supernatural, and thus attributeless, may seem to reduce God to nothingness. As a friend exclaimed, 'Surely, God is more than just attributeless!' But how could that be true? What is attributeless (and *only* what is attributeless) is unlimited, infinite, greater-than-the-greatest, supreme, perfect (i.e., complete and flawless), and so on. Practically all of the typical attributes of God follow from, and cohere with, the fact that God is attributeless. So, by accepting that God is attributeless, I do not take away anything from God. In fact, it is only by accepting that God is attributeless (i.e., nothing in particular) that we can see that God is infinite (i.e., all in essence).

Similarly, that God is supernatural, and thus attributeless, may seem to reduce religion to cold-blooded philosophy. But, again, it does not. First of all, because true philosophy is not cold-blooded at all. Second, because by arguing for this path of reason, I am not arguing against other (religious) paths. This path is just one of many. All paths have the same goal. The paths do not contradict each other and can even be mutually supportive. So, I am actually upgrading religion by adding a path of reason. Third, because a path of reason may help religions to remain relevant in this age of reason. The success of science decreased our faith in dogma, but it also increased our faith in reason. By offering a path of reason, religions can benefit from this increased faith in reason.

On a more personal level: If God is supernatural, God is not causal and thus cannot help us in the way we imagined (e.g., protect us, comfort us, love us, i.e., help us deal with the consequences of sin), but realizing that God is supernatural does set us free (e.g., free from the need for help, protection, comfort, love, i.e., free from sin). If God is supernatural, God cannot give us absolution (i.e., forgive our sins and spare us the consequences of our sins), but realizing that God is supernatural does result in salvation (i.e., freedom from sin and the consequences of sin, a return to paradise as it was before we ate the fruit from the tree of knowledge). If God is supernatural, we cannot get closer to God, but realizing that

God is supernatural means that we *are* God (i.e., it is divine union, apotheosis, the end of separation). And is that not what religion is ultimately about?

Appendix 2: Supernatural vs natural

There are roughly two "schools of thought" regarding God:

1. The natural school of thought. It is popular in natural theology and in the philosophy of religion. This school of thought proceeds by natural means (e.g., as much as possible in accordance with contemporary methods and standards of rationality as they are used in the natural sciences) and thus cannot deal with God as supernatural (or so most people thought).
2. The supernatural school. It is popular in theology. This school of thought considers God to be supernatural but cannot proceed by natural means (or so most people thought). Instead, it relies on supernatural means, e.g., divine revelation.

There seemed to be an unbridgeable gap between the two because the natural and supernatural are of completely different orders. But this natural account of God as supernatural bridges the apparent gap between natural and supernatural theology and philosophy. The gap between the natural sciences (which rely on natural means and thus seem incapable of dealing with God as supernatural) and supernatural theology (which can deal with God as supernatural but relies on supernatural means, e.g., divine revelation). Thus, the account can be seen as a special kind of natural theory, one that allows for God as supernatural, or the account can be seen as a special kind of supernatural theory, one that proceeds by natural means.

Appendix 3: Ideas, propositions, claims, statements, and sentences.

A proposition is an idea. A proposition can be expressed in a claim, i.e., statement, sentence. I use the words 'claim' and 'statement' and 'sentence' interchangeably. A proposition can often be expressed by different claims. For example, the claim that 'God is supernatural', the claim that 'what is not supernatural, is not what is God', and the claim that 'being supernatural is a necessary condition for being God', all express the same proposition (where the latter two are more accurate in that they avoid allegations of existential import, but the first is linguistically more convenient).

Appendix 4: Notion, concept, and nature of God

I use the odd phrase 'notion of God' instead of the more common 'concept of God' and 'nature of God' because, as we have seen, if God is supernatural, God is not conceptual, and God does not have a nature (i.e., essential properties).

Appendix 5: Existential import and circularity

A statement has existential import if the truth of the statement depends on (the belief in) the existence of the referents of one or more of its terms. Thus, a statement that has existential import, assumes the existence of the referents of one or more of its terms. This causes no confusion in case of statements that have explicit existential import, like 'God exists'. But it can cause confusion in case of statements that may have implicit existential import, like 'God is supernatural'. The latter has implicit existential import if one believes it cannot be true unless God exists.

In arguments for the existence of the referents of their terms, such (hidden) implicit existential import can lead to (hidden) vicious circularity. This occurs if the truth of the conclusion depends on the implicit existential import in one or more of the premises. If it does, the argument may commit the logical fallacy known as *petitio principii*, 'assuming the conclusion', also, somewhat confusingly, known as 'begging the question'.

Some people believe this to be the case here, especially where I argue that God *is* (i.e., in chapter 9). They believe that proposition [1] has existential import and that the argument that God *is*, is therefore circular. But neither is the case:

1) Proposition [1] is the idea that 'what is not supernatural, is not what is God'. This claim is generally not considered to have existential import. Nor should it in this case. It is only when we forget that the statement that 'God is supernatural' is but a simplified (contrapositive) version of the original statement, that it can be (mis)taken to have existential import.

2) Even if proposition [1] had existential import, the argument would not be circular because the truth of the conclusion does not depend on the supposed existential import in proposition [1]. Instead, the existence of God is derived from the existence of the one and only supernatural, which is derived from the existence of referential equivalents (e.g., *being*, consciousness, and what I am).

Appendix 6: Adjective or noun?

I may sometimes seem to equivocate between the use of the adjective 'supernatural' and the noun '(the) supernatural'. If I do, it is harmless because of what is supernatural, there cannot be more than one, so what is supernatural is the only one of its kind, so it is necessarily identical with that. The adjective (supernatural) only applies to the noun (i.e., the supernatural), so, the adjective and the noun both refer to the one and only supernatural.

Appendix 7: Predicating or identifying?

Although many claims in this account of God may seem predicative, most of the claims are in fact identity claims (in the strong sense of numerical identity, total qualitative identity, being exactly and unconditionally the same). I allow the ambivalence for a number of reasons:

1) Because it does not hurt if the claims are (initially) interpreted as predicative. The predicative interpretation is sufficient for most arguments, and it often makes the claims more acceptable.

2) Because the predicative form is less unwieldy. For example, the claim that 'God is supernatural' is less unwieldy than 'What the term God signifies is numerically identical to what the term supernatural signifies'.

3) Because it is easier to read. The "attributes" of God are typically used as predicates and using them differently sounds odd. I would have to say, 'God is identical with *the* supernatural' or 'God is identical with what is supernatural' and explain what I mean with 'identical'.

Appendix 8: Theology, Philosophy, Psychology

Part I of this account is probably one of the most purely philosophical accounts of God. It does not rely on scripture or exegesis, but merely on the notion of God that is shared by practically everybody, regardless of their religion or denomination, if any, and regardless of whether they believe that God exists. However, a truly philosophical account of what (theistic) religions call God, would be an account of *being* (and would not even use the word God). This is the subject-matter of first philosophy, the study of *being* (qua *being*). If we separate (theistic) religion from philosophy, we get:

Table 3: Religion and philosophy

	Religion	Philosophy
The key topic:	God	*Being*
The study:	Theology	First philosophy
The goal:	Divine union, salvation from sin and the consequences of sin (e.g., toil, pain, suffering)	Wisdom, salvation from ignorance and the consequences of ignorance (e.g., doubt, suffering)

First philosophy, the study of *being*, is the philosophical counterpart of theology, the study of God. Philosophy of religion is not the philosophical counterpart of theology. Philosophy of religion is the study of religion(s) and concerns itself with the question whether God exists, but does not study God itself.

Where 'God' is the key notion of religions, '*being*' is the key notion of philosophy. Roughly: Metaphysics and ontology are about what *is* (and what *is* not). and about what it is that *is*. Epistemology is about how we can know that what *is*, *is*, and that what *is* not, *is* not. Ethics is about what ought to *be*. The key notion in all is *being*.

Strangely enough, however, philosophy does not know where to start when it comes to '*being*'. It tends to get side-tracked even before it gets started. Parmenides may have got it right, but besides a few fragments of his own work and some third person accounts, it is not enough. Aristotle makes a promising start, notices *being*, confirms its importance, considers it to be the subject-proper of philosophy, defines 'first philosophy' as 'the study of *being* qua *being*', equates first philosophy with theology, and so on, but then leaves it at that. Instead he goes off to studying the supposed *being* of beings, of things that *appear to be*. He goes about that very cleverly but misses the central point of philosophy. Others followed Aristotle's lead, with the possible exception of a few.

A similar thing seems to have happened in psychology, the study of the psyche. 'Psyche' (i.e., anima, soul, consciousness) is referentially equivalent with 'God' and '*being*', but that is not what psychology studies. Psychology studies (the) mind. To be taken seriously as a proper (natural) science, psychology needed a suitable (natural) topic. The psyche is not a suitable topic because it is supernatural (and thus cannot be studied in the way one can study a natural phenomenon). But mind (i.e., the sense faculty for mental phenomena, e.g., thoughts, feelings, and perceptions) is a suitable topic. Mind may not be the psyche, but it is also non-physical and therefore close enough. And (the functioning of) mind can be studied empirically, according to the scientific method, according to the standards and methods that apply to the natural sciences, i.e., scientifically. Moreover the study of (the) mind is also interesting and important, albeit only relatively. In summary, in its drive to be taken seriously as a proper (natural) science, psychology has lost sight of its subject-proper, the psyche, which is supernatural. To gain the world, it had to lose its soul.

Table 4: Religion, philosophy, psychology

	Religion	Philosophy	Psychology
The key topic:	God	*Being*	Psyche
The study:	Theology	First philosophy	Psychology
The goal:	Salvation Divine union	Wisdom True knowledge	Happiness End suffering

So, theology may not provide understandable answers, but philosophy and psychology seem to be missing the point altogether, although *being* and the psyche can be studied empirically and arguably scientifically. The crux is that we should not treat non-conceptual notions as if they were conceptual. We can deal rationally, empirically, and scientifically with non-conceptual notions, but not by demanding that they be conceptual, that they have conceptual attributes. We have to go about it in a different way, e.g.:
- by identifying them with other (familiar) notions (i.e., referential equivalents).
- by saying what they are not (e.g., *via negativa, neti neti*).
- by means of non-categorical logics. (Perhaps propositional logic? Identity logic?)
Besides these rational, scientific ways of dealing with non-conceptual notions, there are also other ways, e.g.:
- by means of devotion,

- by means of prayer,
- by means of meditation (i.e., non-conceptual realization by direct-seeing, e.g., *vipassana*).

Appendix 9: Logical equivalents

Here is a series of claims that are logically equivalent with the basic claim that:
1. God is supernatural.
That is, that:
2. What is not supernatural, is not what is God.
3. Being supernatural is a necessary condition for being God.
4. If X is God, X is supernatural.
In general terms:
5. God is outside and above all else (i.e., all except God).
6. God is outside and above all things (but not outside and above all).[1]
7. God is outside and above everything (i.e., 'all things', i.e., 'all else').
8. God is outside and above all phenomena.[2]
9. God is outside and above all that appears.
10. God is outside and above all that appears to be.
11. God is outside and above all that appears to me.
12. God is outside and above all distinguishing features.
13. God is outside and above all that is object (to me) because God is subject ('I').
In less general terms:
14. God is outside and above the creation.
15. God is outside and above the apparent reality.
16. God is outside and above my life (waking as well as dream life).
17. God is outside and above the content of consciousness.
Categorically:

---

[1] Please do not take the term "things" to imply a belief in things-in-themselves, i.e., objectively real things, things that also exist in some other way than as an appearance. Neither physical or mental things.

[2] Regardless of whether phenomena are taken to be mere appearances or to be caused by things-in-themselves (e.g., perceptions, (re)presentations, after-images of things-in-themselves).

18. God is outside and above all that is physical and/or mental.
19. God is outside and above space, time, causality,
    and outside and above everything in space, time, causality.
20. God is absolutely transcendent, supreme.
21. God is above the highest (i.e., higher-than-the-highest).
22. God is below the lowest (i.e., lower-than-the-lowest).
23. God is further-than-the-furthest.
24. God is nearer-than-the-nearest.
25. God is bigger-than-the-biggest (i.e., larger-than-the-largest).
26. God is greater-than-the-greatest.
27. God is smaller-than-the-smallest.
28. God is earlier-than-the-earliest.
29. God is later-than-the-latest.
In terms of things, phenomena, objects, etc.:
30. God is not a thing (but *being*).
31. God is not a phenomenon (i.e., not an appearance).
32. God does not appear (but is that which all else appears to).
33. God does not *appear to be* (but *is*).
34. God does not appear to me (but is what I am).
35. God is not object (to me) (but is the subject (that I am)).
36. God is not content of consciousness (but consciousness itself).
37. God neither is nor has a distinguishing feature (i.e., property).
38. God is neither physical nor mental (but meta-physical and meta-mental, i.e., spiritual, neutral).
39. God is neither temporal, nor spatial, nor causal (but simply *is*, here and now).

Appendix 10: Why 'supernatural' instead of 'simple' or 'perfect' or other candidates?

Why an account of God as 'supernatural' and not as 'simple', or 'perfect', or any of the other (logically equivalent) notions of God, like the ones in the previous appendix, and like Love, Mercy, Grace, Truth, Holy Spirit, Supreme Being, Creator, Lord, Greatest, Almighty, Absolute, or One. (These words a usually capitalized. Perhaps to stress the holy or absolute sense in which they apply to God instead of the relative sense in which they apply to natural things? I am not sure but follow custom simply to avoid disrespecting anybody.

Why supernatural?

The question 'Why supernatural?' was actually already answered in the chapter, 'Is it successful?'. To recapitulate the reasons:

1. The basic notion is readily and widely acceptable.
   - ○ Practically everybody considers (their) God to be supernatural.
   - ○ It is intuitive. ('Of course, God is supernatural!')
   - ○ It is not *prima facie* contradictory. ('If God is supernatural, of course God appears to be supernatural and have all of the supernatural attributes'.)
   - ○ That 'what is God, is what is supernatural' may well be analytic.
2. The account is coherent.
   - ○ It is a uniform whole.
   - ○ It is internally consistent.
   - ○ It is externally consistent.
3. The account is complete.
   - ○ It approaches the matter from all possible angles.

Also:

4. The account deals with the issue of God's existence.
   - ○ That God exists follows from the fact that God is supernatural.
5. The basic notion is clear, unambiguous, informative.
   - ○ It is clear: 'Supernatural' means 'outside and above the natural', i.e., 'outside and above all that is born, created, caused, or otherwise conditioned'.
   - ○ It is unambiguous: It has a single meaning (if perhaps not always correctly understood and/or used).
   - ○ It is informative: 'Supernatural' immediately explains:
     - ▪ What is opposed to what (i.e., natural vs. supernatural).
     - ▪ What it is that God transcends (i.e., the natural).
     - ▪ That God's transcendence is absolute (i.e., that God is outside the natural).
     - ▪ Which "attributes" God has (i.e., all supernatural "attributes") and does not have (i.e., no natural attributes).

Why not 'simple'?

If God is supernatural, God is attributeless, and thus absolutely simple. In this absolute sense, the claim that 'God is simple' is logically equivalent with the claim that 'God is supernatural'. Both express the same proposition (i.e., idea). So, why prefer 'supernatural' over 'simple'? Because:

1. The basic notion is not readily and widely acceptable.
   o Practically nobody considers (his/her) God to be simple.
   o It is counterintuitive. ('God simple? You must be joking!')
   o It is *prima facie* contradictory. ('How can God be simple yet have many attributes?')
5. The basic notion is not clear, unambiguous, or informative.
   o 'Simple' is not clear or unambiguous. It can mean, for example:
     ▪ plain, basic, or uncomplicated in form, nature, or design, without much decoration or ornamentation;
     ▪ easily understood or done, presenting no difficulty;
     ▪ humble and unpretentious, lacking intelligence;
     ▪ not compound, without parts, indivisible, one.

   Even if we limit the meaning of 'simple' to the kind of meaning that may be intended here, we can ask if 'simple' means:
     ▪ without attributes (i.e., absolutely simple) or
     ▪ with just one or a few attributes (i.e., relatively simple)?

   If the difference seems marginal, please note it is crucial:
     ▪ If 'simple' means 'absolutely simple, attributeless', it is referentially equivalent with 'supernatural' and the account of God as simple will cohere with the account of God as supernatural. However, if 'simple' means 'relatively simple, with one or just a few attributes', it is the very opposite of 'supernatural' and the accounts will contradict each other throughout. Unfortunately, the relative sense of 'simple' is the more common.
     ▪ If 'simple' means 'absolutely simple, attributeless', an account of God as simple removes all doubt with regard to God's existence, in the same way as the account of God as supernatural does. However, if 'simple' means 'relatively simple, with one or just a few attributes', it does not, and cannot, because a God that is relatively simple, is not supernatural, and not God. Unfortunately, the relative sense of 'simple' is the more common.

The point here is not to give an exhaustive list of the possible meanings of 'simple' but just to show that it has several meanings, and that the different meanings can lead to misunderstandings and confusion.

o 'Simple' is not informative, at least not as informative as 'supernatural'. For example, it does not immediately explain:

- What is opposed to what (i.e., simple vs ...?).
- What it is that God transcends.
- That God's transcendence is absolute.
- If God has no attributes or if God has one or a few attributes.

Thus, the claim that 'God is simple' is less suitable as the basic proposition for an account of God than the claim that 'God is supernatural'.

Why not 'divine simplicity'?

The doctrine of divine simplicity is a dominant account of God. Although the basic claim, 'God is simple', may be correct, the proposition is confusing (i.e., the meaning is not clear and unambiguous, e.g., 'divine simplicity' is sometimes understood as 'relative simplicity, e.g., with one attribute only' rather than as 'absolute simplicity, without any attributes'), counterintuitive ('God is simple? You must be joking!'), and *prima facie* contradictory ('How can God be simple yet have many attributes?'). Thus, an account of God as simple will continuously provoke objections and questions.

In theory, the resulting objections and questions can be dealt with easily. By explaining that 'simple' is to be understood in its absolute sense, as attributeless, and not in its relative sense, as having only one or a few attributes. But this explanation is not widely and readily acceptable. Neither to opponents of the doctrine of divine simplicity, nor to proponents. Most seem convinced that God is more than just attributeless. They have not yet realized that that is impossible because only a God that is attributeless is truly infinite, supreme, greater-than-the-greatest, perfect, has the other typical "attributes" of God, and truly qualifies as God. It may also be that they did not notice that the so-called "attributes" of God are not real, natural, categorical, conceptual attributes, but supernatural, transcategorical, transconceptual "attributes". Whatever the reasons, it results in them trying to prove the impossible: that God is supernatural yet truly has (real, natural, conceptual) attributes.

As a result, the objections and questions have been dealt with in many different ways. This has cluttered, fragmented, and confused the doctrine of divine simplicity. Ironically, by now, most variants of the doctrine of divine simplicity appear to have but one thing in common: being over-complicated. Even general introductions to the doctrine of divine simplicity (e.g., on SEP, IEP, and Wikipedia) are mind-goggling. And at least some versions have been corrupted (e.g., adopting 'simple' in its relative sense, endowing God with one or more (real) attributes).

Under the circumstances, it seems that any attempt to repair the doctrine of divine simplicity can only lead to further confusion. As a uniform account of God, it seems beyond repair. So, instead of trying to repair it, it may be time for a successor. Especially now that there is a promising candidate: The account of God as supernatural.

The account of God a supernatural also claims that God is simple, but it does so in a manner that is intuitive ('Of course, God is supernatural!') and consistent ('If God is supernatural, of course God has all these supernatural "attributes"!'). So, the account of God as supernatural instantly overcomes the primary weaknesses of the doctrine of divine simplicity. Therewith, it prevents the obvious objections and questions that continue to plague the doctrine of divine simplicity and that inevitably clutter, fragment, and confuse it.

The account of God as supernatural also has some other advantages over the doctrine of divine simplicity: It clearly explains what sets God apart from all else (i.e., God is supernatural; all else is natural) and what it is that God transcends (i.e., God transcends the natural). And it removes all doubt with regard to God's existence, because the supernatural demonstrably exists. Last but not least, while the doctrine of divine simplicity is a theological, predominantly Christian doctrine, the account of God as supernatural could well become a philosophical and universally acceptable account of God and the 'ultimate' of non-theistic religions.

In summary, the account of God as supernatural seems to be a suitable successor to the doctrine of divine simplicity.

Why not 'perfect'?

If God is supernatural, God is attributeless, and thus absolutely perfect (i.e., complete and flawless). In this absolute sense, the claim that 'God is perfect' is logically equivalent with the claim that 'God is supernatural'. Both express the same proposition (i.e., idea). So, why do I prefer 'supernatural' over 'perfect'? Because 'perfect' can be understood in different ways, some of which are problematic. For example, because 'perfect' (from Latin *perficio*) means 'bring to an end' and (logically) implies 'incapable of change', and thus ends up as meaning something like 'dead', which is usually not what we want to say of God. Also, because perfection seems to require imperfection, e.g., in case of perfect beauty, and may seem to be a contradictory concept.

Thus, the claim that 'God is perfect' is less suitable as the basic proposition for an account of God than the claim that 'God is supernatural'.

Why not 'perfect being theology'?

Perfect Being Theology ('PBT') is another dominant account of God. Although the claim that God is perfect (i.e. absolutely perfect) is correct, this is not what PBT says (or, at least, what I here take it to say). PBT says that God is 'the most perfect being' (i.e., relatively perfect) or subtle variants thereof, e.g.: 'the most perfect being possible', 'the most perfect being that could be', 'the most perfect being that could be conceived', or *aliquid quo nihil maius cogitari possit* (which roughly translates as 'something than which nothing greater can be conceived').

But, if God is supernatural, God is perfect (i.e., absolutely perfect) and not just the most perfect being possible (i.e., comparable, relatively perfect). If God is supernatural, God is not the greatest, but greater-than-the-greatest; God is not a *primus inter pares* (i.e., a first among equals, the greatest of all natural things) but super-natural (i.e., outside and above all equals, greater than all natural things). This is the very point about God, that which makes God God.

So, if PBT claimed that God is perfect (i.e., absolutely perfect), it would be compatible with AGS. But PBT claims that God is the most perfect (i.e., only relatively perfect), which is incompatible with the notion that God is supernatural, and thus perfect (i.e., absolutely perfect).

So, if God is supernatural, PBT is mistaken.

Why not 'attributeless'?

The claim that 'God is attributeless' is logically equivalent with the claim that 'God is supernatural'. The two claims express the same proposition (i.e., idea). So, why not use 'attributeless' as the basic notion of God? Because:
1. 'Attributeless' is possibly even less intuitive than 'simple'.
2. 'Attributeless' seems prone to trigger a similar kind of confusion as 'simple'. Where 'simple' could be understood in its absolute sense (of being attributeless) and in its relative sense (of having just one or a few attributes), 'attributeless' can be correctly understood as 'without natural attributes', but it can also be understood as 'without natural *and supernatural* "attributes"'.

Thus, 'attributeless' is not a suitable notion of God to serve as the basis for an account of God.

Why not 'transcendent'?

The claim that 'God is transcendent' is logically equivalent with the claim that 'God is supernatural'. The two claims express the same proposition (i.e., idea). So, why not use 'transcendent' as the basic notion of God? Because supernatural is more informative. 'Supernatural' also tells us:

1. what God transcends (i.e. the natural, all else, everything), and
2. that God is absolutely transcendent (i.e., outside and above the natural, outside and above all else, outside and above all things).

Transcendent does not. Therefore, 'supernatural' beats 'transcendent'.

Why not '*being*'?

The claim that 'God is *being*', e.g., that 'God is supreme *being*', is logically equivalent with the claim that 'God is supernatural'. The two claims express the same proposition (i.e., idea). '*Being*' is an interesting alternative for a variety of reasons. For me personally, because it is the subject-matter of first philosophy (the study of *being* qua *being* for the love of wisdom) which is my primary area of interest. But also because of several important scriptural references to God as *being* (e.g., I am that I *am*) and because the view of God as supreme *being* is quite established. So, why not use '*being*' as the basic notion of God? Because it cannot measure up to supernatural when it comes to dealing with God. It is not intuitive. *Being* has a long history of being misunderstood (e.g., as a universal applying to "beings" that *are* not but merely *appear to be*) and is often still considered to be equivocal and vacuous.

Why not 'consciousness'?

The claim that 'God is consciousness' is logically equivalent with the claim that 'God is supernatural'. The two claims express the same proposition (i.e., idea). 'Consciousness' is again an interesting alternative for a variety of reasons. For me personally, because it is the subject matter of Consciousnism (i.e., first philosophy in terms of consciousness). So, why not use 'consciousness' as the basic notion of God? Because the meaning of the term is controversial. There is a lot of confusion about consciousness. (Perhaps even more than about God.) So, it will not be helpful.

Why not 'the self'?

Despite strong scriptural support (especially in Hindu, but also in Abrahamic scriptures), the notion that 'I am God' is completely unacceptable, considered to be blasphemy, and triggers abusive letters and even threats. (Not much seems to have changed since Jesus said that he and the father were one, and they accused him of blasphemy and wanted to stone him. See John 10:30.)

Printed in Great Britain
by Amazon

21237556R00078